TQManager

Warren H. Schmidt
Jerome P. Finnigan

TQManager

*A Practical Guide
for Managing in a
Total Quality
Organization*

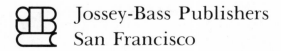
Jossey-Bass Publishers
San Francisco

Substantial discounts on bulk quantities of Jossey-Bass books are available to corporations, professional associations, and other organizations. For details and discount information, contact the special sales department at Jossey-Bass Inc., Publishers. (415) 433-1740; Fax (415) 433-0499.

For international orders, please contact your local Paramount Publishing International office.

Manufactured in the United States of America

The paper used in this book is acid-free and meets the State of California requirements for recycled paper (50 percent recycled waste, including 10 percent postconsumer waste), which are the strictest guidelines for recycled paper currently in use in the United States.

10% POST CONSUMER WASTE

Library of Congress Cataloging-in-Publication Data

Schmidt, Warren H.
    TQManager : a practical guide for managing in a total quality organization / Warren H. Schmidt and Jerome P. Finnigan.
        p.   cm. — (The Jossey-Bass management series)
    Includes bibliographical references and index.
    ISBN 1-55542-559-3 (alk. paper)
    1. Total quality management.   I. Finnigan, Jerome P., date.
    II. Title.   III. Series.
    HD62.15.S363   1993
    658.5′62—dc20

                                                                93-4588
                                                                CIP

FIRST EDITION
HB Printing   10 9 8 7 6 5 4 3 2   Code 9380

The Jossey-Bass
Management Series

*We dedicate this book
to America's middle managers,
whose good sense and readiness to learn
are so essential to the quality and success
of the organizations they serve.*

CONTENTS

PREFACE

So it's finally happened! Your organization is going for TQM. There were rumors first, then it became official. From now on the watchword is *quality*, and that watchword has a clear, simple definition: *customer satisfaction*.

You had heard and read about Total Quality Management before, but you had never really taken the time to get into the nuts and bolts of it. Now, however, you realize that your career depends on becoming an effective TQManager. That means understanding what this new approach to management is all about, how it affects your role as a manager, and what particular competencies you must acquire or sharpen.

A WORD TO THE READER
ABOUT THIS BOOK

The purpose of *TQManager* is to give you a crash course in Total Quality Management. We surveyed working TQManagers about what they need to know to succeed in a Total Quality organization, and, from our sample of successful and unsuccessful managers, we have learned which concepts and competencies TQManagers must use in order to survive, contribute, and advance in their organizations. We have boiled these concepts and competencies down to the basics to make the information more easily available.

We've organized the book into three parts. Part One deals with the concepts the TQManager needs to know about TQM and the many challenges it poses. Part Two presents the five key TQManagerial competencies and shows why they're important and how they can be developed. The third part offers resources that help you assess your managerial style and lists sources of help for your personal continual improvement.

OUR "CUSTOMERS"

We intend *TQManager* to be useful to a wide range of managers. Our primary audience consists of those who are part of a Total Quality organization and want to get a more solid understanding of how they can be most effective in their changing role. This crash course in TQM should also be useful to any manager who is about to join a Total Quality organization, as well as to executives, administrators, and managers who are considering Total Quality for their organizations but aren't certain about what will be expected of them.

As you begin your journey, we want to congratulate you. You and your organization have now joined the Quality Revolution—the most significant shift in American management thought and practice since the Industrial Revolution a century ago. Be ready to learn new ways to approach your job and deal with your colleagues. It can be a fresh adventure for everyone in your organization, and it may well determine your chance to survive in a rapidly changing and increasingly competitive world.

Los Angeles, California   Warren H. Schmidt
July 1993   Jerome P. Finnigan

THE AUTHORS

Warren H. Schmidt is professor emeritus of public administration at the University of Southern California. He received his A.B. degree (1942) from Wayne State University in journalism, his M.Div. degree (1945) from Concordia Theological Seminary in St. Louis, and his Ph.D. degree (1949) from Washington University in psychology. He served on the faculties of the University of Missouri, Union College, and Springfield College before joining the faculty at the University of California, Los Angeles (UCLA) in 1955, where he held a number of administrative and faculty positions, including director of the Unified MBA Program and dean of executive education in the Graduate School of Management. He was granted emeritus status when he left UCLA in 1976 to join the faculty of the School of Public Administration at the University of Southern California.

Schmidt's writings and teaching in leadership, group dynamics, and organization development have been directed toward making organizations more productive and satisfying places to work. He is author of several books and more than one hundred articles. One of his articles, "How to Choose a Leadership Pattern" (coauthored with Robert Tannenbaum for the *Harvard Business Review*), was designated an HBR

Classic and has sold more than one million offprints. He has also been the writer or adviser for more than seventy management and educational films. One of his animated films, *Is It Always Right to Be Right?* won an Academy Award in 1971 and was named Training Film of the Decade by the Industrial Film Board in 1980.

In addition to his academic work, Schmidt has served as chair of the Los Angeles County Economy and Efficiency Commission and currently is a member of the Los Angeles City Quality and Productivity Commission. He is a past board member of the NTL Institute and the board of governors of the American Society for Training and Development. He is a certified psychologist in California and a diplomate of the American Board of Professional Psychology. He has conducted executive and management seminars throughout the United States and abroad.

Jerome P. Finnigan is human resources manager for Xerox Corporation's Systems Competency Unit. He earned his A.B. degree (1959) from the University of San Francisco in English and was an intern in public affairs (1960) with the Coro Foundation. He joined Xerox in 1966 and has held a variety of human resource positions in Los Angeles and Rochester, New York.

Finnigan's assignments have largely been in human resource development and organization development. He was an early advocate of quality circles in the late 1970s and was acting quality officer for the printing systems division during Xerox's implementation of Total Quality. He is a frequent lecturer at UCLA on Total Quality Management.

Finnigan is affiliated with the American Society for Training and Development and the National Alliance of Business. He is past chair of the California Business Consortium for Management in Education and was a member of the state committee that wrote California's *Strategic Plan for Educational Options in the Twenty-First Century: Roads to the Future*. Finnigan also served on the committee of the National Center for Research in Vocational Education, which drafted

New Designs for the Comprehensive High School for the U.S. Department of Education. He is currently a member of California's Adult Education Steering Committee.

Warren H. Schmidt and Jerome P. Finnigan are coauthors of *The Race Without a Finish Line: America's Quest for Total Quality* (1992).

TQManager

PART ONE

WHAT YOU NEED TO KNOW ABOUT TQM

As managers we develop our perception of our bosses, subordinates, and colleagues over a period of years. We acquire a whole range of assumptions, attitudes, and strategies for handling our responsibilities and getting the job done. We find what works and what fails in our dealings with the rest of the organization. Our theory of management works for us most of the time.

When a new management theory comes along, we are both curious and skeptical. When we are asked to change our behavior, that curiosity and skepticism is intensified. This is now *serious* — and maybe even a bit threatening.

Total Quality Management is a new way of thinking about organizations and how people should relate and work in them. It's natural and sensible to ask a lot of questions, ranging from "What is TQM?" to "What am I supposed to do differently in a TQManaged organization?"

This first part tries to answer these two basic questions. The first chapter is designed to give you an overview of TQM and to help you understand why it has gained such popularity in the management community. We also deal with questions like "What do I have to learn that is new?" and "Are there management theories and practices that I should discard?"

The second chapter focuses on what TQM means to you as a manager and on the challenges it poses to you in your approach to your job. We'll discuss some of the background of TQM, but mostly we'll focus on what is required of the TQManager—the manager who functions effectively in an organization committed to Total Quality Management.

Welcome to the wondrous world of TQM, and to some exciting new ways to think about your job, your colleagues, and your organization!

1

Understanding the Concept

When your chief executive or your boss tells you, "We're going to implement Total Quality Management in this organization," it's natural to ask a number of questions, like "What is TQM, anyway?" "What made them decide to pursue *this* approach to management?" "What's wrong with what we've been doing all these years?" "Is this something I should take seriously, or is it another one of those management fads that is likely to be replaced by something else in the future?"

If your key executives have done their homework, you can be pretty sure that life in your organization is going to change significantly in the upcoming months and years. You and your colleagues will be expected to relate differently and communicate differently than you have in the past. Methods of evaluating work and making decisions will change. Priorities will shift. Most important of all, adopting TQM as the guiding philosophy for your organization also means that you will have a better chance to survive and flourish in the twenty-first century. (The reason for this is spelled out more fully in Chapter Two.)

As part of our preparation for writing this book, we asked executives from TQManaged public and private organizations in various parts of the country to identify middle managers who seemed particularly successful in adjusting to the TQM way of operation. We asked these managers about their first reactions to TQM and how TQM changed the way they do their jobs. We asked them what new concepts or skills they had to learn and how they apportion their time to their various responsibilities. We also asked them what advice they would give to managers in organizations that are becoming—or are about to become—TQManaged.

Our survey and interviews of managers who have successfully made the transition to TQM indicate that TQManagers want to know the answers to these questions:

1. What are the basic ideas behind TQM?
2. How is TQM different from traditional management?
3. What are the stumbling blocks that a TQManager should know about?
4. Why has TQM become so popular?
5. Why has TQM succeeded in some organizations and failed in others?

WHAT ARE THE BASIC IDEAS BEHIND TQM?

As you become a TQManager, you will want to be clear on the underlying assumptions and guiding principles of TQM and what they mean for the way you approach your job. You will discover that some beliefs about how work gets done are no longer valid, while others have become more important. After surveying many managers who have made a successful transition to TQM behavior, we found that it is important to have a solid understanding of the following basic concepts:

■ Organizations are made up of a complex system of customers and suppliers, with every individual executive, manager, and worker functioning as both a supplier and a customer.

- Quality—meeting the customer's requirements—is the priority goal and is presumed to be the key to organizational survival and growth.

- Continuous improvement is the guiding principle. This goes for the product or service you produce and for your own competence on the job; TQM organizations are *learning* organizations and depend on their people becoming increasingly competent and creative.

- Teams and groups are primary vehicles for planning and problem solving.

- Developing relationships of openness and trust among members of the organization at all levels is the key condition for success.

Let's discuss each of these ideas and ask why they've gotten so much attention in the last decade. In the second part of this book we describe how your behavior as a manager will change, but for now, let's just get a clear understanding of how to think about your TQManaged organization.

Your Organization Is a Complex System of Customers and Suppliers

Many people, when asked to describe their organization, will begin to draw an organizational chart or talk about divisions and departments, lines of authority, and bosses and subordinates. In TQManaged organizations, people are more likely to pay attention to who supplies them with what they need to do their job and who the customer is for what they produce. In a company that has a fleet of trucks, truck drivers are the customers of mechanics who service their trucks. To improve service to the drivers, the mechanics interview them and determine their expectations about schedules and the type of work to be done. In turn, the mechanics are the customers of the parts and supplies departments, which routinely ask them about their expectations for timely delivery of the right parts. For each transaction there is a supplier and a customer, who may be internal or external. It's a system of interdependent relationships whose effectiveness depends on how well suppliers understand and meet their customers' requirements.

When you think of an organization this way — when everyone becomes concerned about meeting their customers' requirements — many things change. Realistic communication flows more freely because internal customers have to let their suppliers know what they need in order to do their jobs. People who prepare reports try to understand what the readers of those reports (their customers) want to know. And if they need data for those reports from other colleagues in the organization, they have to let those internal suppliers know what kind of data is needed and when. And so it goes throughout the organization, between departments, between individual managers — even between bosses and subordinates. Everybody in the organization is asking, "Who are my customers and what are their requirements?" and "Who are my suppliers and what do they need to know about my needs?"

When the Malcolm Baldrige National Quality Award examiners visited the Cadillac Motor Car Division plant in Detroit, Michigan, they asked a worker who was polishing a bumper, "Who is your customer?" The worker replied, "Do you mean my *internal* customer or my *external* customer?" The examiner said, "Tell us about both," to which the worker responded, "That fellow over there is my internal customer. He gets the clean bumper and puts chrome on it. My external customer is the person who buys the car."

Quality — Meeting the Customer's Requirements — Is the Top Priority

Customers, not engineers or designers or accountants, set the ultimate criteria for quality. Customers are never regarded as people to whom you present your product in a "take it or leave it" spirit. In some ways this is a supreme act of faith — to believe that if customers are satisfied, they will continue to patronize you and your organization will continue to survive. If you succeed in delighting your customers, they will bring others with them and you will flourish; if you can anticipate their needs and satisfy them, you will have achieved the ultimate in quality. Everything the organization does is directed toward this objective!

To put this into perspective, consider the thinking in a traditional organization. Too often, the customer is seen as simply the end target — someone to be persuaded, influenced and even manipulated, if necessary, to buy what you have produced. Some sales representatives pride themselves on tailoring the customer's needs to fit the "solution" they happen to be selling, even when the fit is forced. The old warning, *caveat emptor* ("Let the buyer beware"), is a reminder of practices that predated the Quality Movement but is still a necessary precaution in some situations today. Customers of a TQManaged organization do not waste time worrying about being "sold" something that does not fit their needs.

This goes for internal customers as well. Colleagues do not try to shortchange one another. Problems and projects are less likely to fall between the cracks. Persons filling out reports for another department try to provide the data that is really needed rather than what is easiest to produce. Materials and information are more likely to arrive when they are needed and in the most useful form. When bosses view their subordinates as customers, they ask themselves and their subordinates, "How can we work together to do the job more effectively?"

Frederick W. Smith, CEO of Federal Express Corporation, put it this way in a 1991 speech to his colleagues: "Here's how it works out in our company. . . . A courier's job is to work directly for the customer. . . . Our front-line manager's job is to make the courier's job easier. . . and her manager's job is to make the front-line manager's job easier and so on until you get to me . . . and my job is to do whatever it takes to help all of our people do their best."

Continuous Improvement Is the Guiding Principle

As parents we encourage our children to do their best, but at work we sometimes are willing to settle for just getting by. If the customer doesn't complain, there's no reason to improve. If the boss is satisfied, it must be okay. "If it ain't broke, don't fix it" is the guiding principle.

In TQManaged organizations, it's different. The standard operating procedure is to keep doing better. As long as things are not perfect, there's room for improvement: new products can get to market faster, new adjustments in processes can cut down on time and cost, and the environment for work can be made more satisfying.

David Kearns, as CEO of Xerox Corporation, told his colleagues, "Quality is a race without a finish line. A focus on quality has made Xerox a stronger company, but we know we'll never be as good as we can be, because we'll always try to be better. We are on a mission of continuous quality improvement" (1991, p. 9).

Teams and Groups Are Primary Vehicles for Planning and Problem Solving

In many organizations *meetings* and *groups* are derogatory words. They conjure up images of boredom, wasted time, and lack of accomplishment. People go to meetings expecting few results and all too often they leave with those expectations met in a self-fulfilling prophecy. In TQManaged organizations, by contrast, teams and groups are seen as essential elements of the organization's operation. Everybody is trained to plan and participate in groups. The result is that meetings become vehicles for creative problem solving, planning, and learning. When groups work well they provide a level of satisfaction that energizes and inspires their members.

In some organizations, everybody gets training in how to plan and participate in meetings and they learn a common set of guidelines for conducting a meeting. The result is that within the first five minutes of any meeting, the following will have been accomplished: (1) the goals and agenda will be clear, (2) a determination will have been made that the right people are in the room to achieve that objective, (3) a discussion leader will have been designated, and (4) someone will have been appointed to keep notes, another to be the "scribe" for the newsprint pad, and another to be particularly sensitive to the group process.

TQManaged organizations also recognize and reward teams, rather than just individuals. When a team solves a problem, every member of the team is recognized. When a group achieves some goal, everyone celebrates. There is little doubt that the exhilaration that comes from being part of a successful team is different from the satisfaction that comes from individual achievement. Setbacks or disappointments are also easier to manage as a member of a team. A final advantage of the team emphasis is a reduction of individual rivalry and distrust, which leads to the next characteristic we want to discuss.

Developing Relationships of Openness and Trust Is a Key Condition for Success

"The single most powerful tool of management is trust," write Sam Culbert and Jack McDonough in their insightful book, *Radical Management* (1985, p. 17). Where trust is high, ideas and communication flow easily. Where trust is low, everything becomes more complicated. People hesitate to point out problems, suggest new ideas, or take responsibility for mistakes. They go to great lengths to create a paper trail to protect their position just in case things go wrong! Many organizations have learned the hard way about the wasted energy that goes into unproductive memos, superfluous copies, and defensive conversations.

In TQManaged organizations, trust is a high priority and is nurtured in a variety of ways. It begins with the communication of organizational goals. Everybody knows what the targets are and how well they are being met. Barriers between divisions and departments are minimized. More work is done in teams, many of which are interdepartmental and cross-functional. Most important of all, errors and problems are viewed as opportunities for learning, rather than as blunders to be punished.

HOW IS TQM DIFFERENT FROM TRADITIONAL MANAGEMENT?

Some of the differences have been alluded to in the previous section, but here we would like to describe point by point the eight major differences we have observed. There is little doubt that the culture of an organization changes when it adopts TQM as its mode of operation. In this section, we focus on the things to look for. After reviewing many charts describing the differences between traditional and TQManaged organizations, we believe that the description produced by the Federal Quality Institute (1991) provides the clearest comparison (Table 1.1).

Organizational Structure: Hierarchical and Rigid Versus Flat and Flexible

Organizations in the past sought stability and dependability; organizations in the 1990s must be responsive and quick. Almost every major reorganization today results in fewer levels of management. There isn't time to send messages up through many layers of a hierarchy to get a decision. Customers want responses right now! Companies that get their products to the marketplace first have the best chance to capture the market. Flexibility is also important to the modern organization. Departmental lines must be overcome or eliminated to solve some kinds of problems.

Attitude Toward Change: Status Quo Versus Continual Improvement

This is one of the most difficult aspects of TQM to sell to Americans. "Continual improvement" does not come easily or naturally to us. We prefer quick, dramatic changes followed by periods of calm. We respond well to crises but when things are operating smoothly, the guideline is "Don't rock the boat." If our customers are still buying and not complaining, why

Table 1.1. Comparison of Traditional and
TQManaged Organizations.

Traditional	TQManaged
The organizational structure is hierarchical and has rigid lines of authority and responsibility.	The organizational structure becomes flatter, more flexible, and less hierarchical.
The focus is on maintaining the status quo ("If it ain't broke, don't fix it").	The focus shifts to continuous improvement in systems and processes (continue to improve it even if it isn't broken).
Workers perceive supervisors as bosses or cops.	Workers perceive supervisors as coaches and facilitators. The manager is seen as a leader.
Supervisor-subordinate relationships are characterized by dependency, fear, and control.	Supervisor-subordinate relationships shift to interdependency, trust, and mutual commitment.
The focus of employee efforts is on individual effort; workers view themselves as competitors.	The focus of employee efforts shifts to team effort; workers see themselves as teammates.
Management perceives labor and training as costs.	Management perceives labor as an asset and training as an investment.
Management determines what quality is and whether it is being provided.	The organization asks customers to define quality and develops measures to determine if customers' requirements are met.
The primary basis for decisions is "gut feeling" or instinct.	The primary basis for decisions shifts to facts and systems.

Source: Federal Quality Institute, 1991, pp. 16–17.

should we worry? Even though most of us would subscribe to the saying that an ounce of prevention is worth a pound of cure, we get more excited about heart transplant operations than disease prevention programs.

TQManagers have to turn this attitude around. They have to sustain their commitment to the day in, day out effort to keep raising the bar and not settle for anything less. Fortunately, it can be done, even in America. Where organizations have succeeded in doing so—places like Motorola,

Xerox, and Federal Express—the results astound even the more optimistic TQMers. Motorola is striving to make products that have only 3.4 defects per million. As they move steadily toward that goal, they have discovered unexpected amounts of pride and fulfillment. But it takes competent management, a topic we'll deal with in Chapter Seven.

Workers' Perception of Their Supervisor: Boss and Cop Versus Coach and Facilitator

Can workers be trusted to do a conscientious job on their own or must they be watched carefully, prodded with rewards, and threatened with punishment? Managers and psychologists have pondered this question for many years with mixed findings. Successful and unsuccessful managers have been on both sides of this issue and can "prove" their conflicting conclusions with dramatic examples. Douglas McGregor (1960) labeled the first group "Theory Y" managers, who assume that workers are essentially trustworthy and that they want to do a good job and be creative. "Theory X" managers, on the other hand, assume that workers are essentially lazy and uncreative and that they want to do as little as possible.

Most American managers are probably somewhere in between, believing that you can trust some workers but have to continually watch and "motivate" others with some combination of rewards and punishments or they will take advantage of the organization. Traditional organizations are likely to lean toward Theory X behavior, using managerial power limited by an increasing array of laws and by restrictions imposed by unions. (An increasing array of laws puts limits on the exercise of that power, and where unions are involved the limits are even stricter.) In general, however, supervisors and managers are expected to be on the side of the organization, rather than on the side of the workers. Workers are to be directed, not "coddled."

TQManagers operate from a strong set of Theory Y assumptions. They view workers as key actors in the organization who will generally use good judgment and act conscientiously if they are given clear goals to achieve and are provided with the necessary skills, knowledge, tools, and authority to do their job. The responsibility of the manager is to make sure that this happens. Managers become coaches to increase workers' competence and facilitators to provide the conditions necessary to do the job. The principal job of the manager is to set realistic goals — usually with the assistance of the worker — and to establish ways to measure progress toward those goals.

Supervisor-Subordinate Relationships: Dependent Versus Interdependent

In the past, workers were often referred to as "hired *hands*," for a very good reason: they were not expected to think, but simply to carry out orders from the boss. The boss got paid to do the thinking and planning and the workers got paid to do what the boss told them to. If the workers were obedient they were rewarded; if they disobeyed they were warned, punished, and ultimately fired. The manager's responsibility was to keep the workers "in line" and productive. All too often, when workers took the initiative to do things differently, their efforts were regarded with suspicion. It was assumed that their inter- est was different from that of the company: they wished only to do as little work as necessary and to maximize their wages, whereas management's interests were to get as much work as possible out of the workers for as little cost as possible. In the traditional organization, this underlying assumption still influ- ences the way bosses and subordinates view one another.

TQManagers operate from a different set of assumptions and therefore their relationship with their subordinates is very different. They assume that subordinates are responsible human beings who will *want* to achieve clear, sensible goals in the most efficient way possible. They also recognize that a manager's effectiveness is dependent on the effectiveness of these colleagues. In addition, TQManagers assume that the people who do the work often have the best ideas on how the work process itself can be improved. The manager needs their input about the resources and equipment required to do the job and the workers need the manager's support in receiving clear goals, authority, and support to do the job. Neither can operate effectively without the other—and they recognize this fact!

This mutual recognition dramatically changes the relationship between supervisor and subordinate. The power to reward or punish is pushed into the background when there is perceived interdependence. The way is therefore open to better communication and a more trusting relationship. In some cases the supervisor acts as the supplier of resources and the subordinate becomes the customer who uses those resources. As in any supplier-customer relationship, the supplier's job is to meet the customer's requirements.

Focus of Employees' Efforts: Individual Versus Team

The American culture emphasizes individual performance. We laud the individual—the hero who risks his life to save a person in distress, the sheriff who stands up to the mob, the courageous entrepreneur who struggles to build a business. It was natural, therefore, for organizations to recognize outstanding individuals who made exceptional contributions to the organization's success.

TQManaged organizations focus more attention on *team* contributions. Although exceptional individuals are sometimes highlighted, more rewards and recognition go to teams. Since more of the solutions to problems and increases in productivity come from groups, it is natural to recognize and reward them, rather than individuals. In this setting, individuals are more likely to view their co-workers as colleagues and teammates, rather than as competitors.

Labor and Training: Cost Versus Asset and Investment

Traditional organizations regard labor as one of their highest costs. When foreign competitors began to take over more market share, the first impulse of some executives was to blame the higher wages of American workers. When unions fight for higher wages, management fights against them on the grounds that the organization will become less competitive. In the same way, training is viewed as an optional expense; when budgets must be cut, it is often the first casualty. The director of training is certainly not the most prestigious position in the traditional organization!

By contrast, TQManaged organizations take seriously the frequently printed statement in annual company reports that "our people are our most important assets." Workers are viewed, not just as the hired hands that do the work, but as the eyes that can see problems and opportunities and the minds that can formulate solutions to problems. Customers are more likely to come in contact with workers than with supervisors, managers, or executives. Jan Carlzon, the president of Scandinavian Airlines Systems, highlighted this fact when he said that the organization's "moments of truth" occur when customers contact employees to get some problem resolved (Carlzon, 1987). These moments determine the customers' impression of the company—and no supervisor is around to make sure that the situation is handled right.

When workers are viewed as assets, training is seen as an investment. As workers' competence grows, the company's worth increases. Efforts are made to keep the training budget intact during difficult times. W. Edwards Deming (1986), America's most noted TQM guru, devoted two of his famous fourteen points for quality management to improving the competence of the work force: "Institute training" and "Encourage education and self-improvement for everyone." The vice president for human resource development is one of the TQManaged organization's most influential executives. (It is interesting to note that in Japanese firms, the officer in charge of human resource development outranks the chief financial officer.)

Determiners of Quality: Managers Versus Customers

In the traditional organization, management decides what the standard of quality should be, based on their assessment of the market and the competition. Once standards have been determined, a process is developed to ensure that the products or services measure up to them. Management often assumes that exceeding these standards is unnecessary and perhaps wasteful. It becomes the task of the sales force to convince the customers that the quality of the product or service is superior to that of the competition.

TQManaged organizations depend upon *customers* to define quality. *They* set the standards that count the most. *They* are the ones who must be satisfied — or even delighted! This is a significant shift of influence that affects everyone in the organization. Those who are closest to the customer — the clerks, the salespersons, the service personnel — become the most valuable sources of data. Their influence in the organization inevitably grows. They are no longer perceived by their colleagues as being at the bottom of the organizational chart. In fact, some companies, like Federal Express and Nordstrom, turned their organizational charts upside down to remind everyone that the top position is occupied by the customers, followed by those who deal directly with them. One significant result is that managers listen more carefully to subordinates, knowing that information gained at the grass roots must travel quickly to planners and strategists. This habit of listening to subordinates also reinforces the climate of interdependence and trust.

Basis of Decisions:
"Gut Feeling" Versus Facts and Systems

In a stable world, experience is a reliable guide to decision making. When a successful, experienced manager or executive says, "This is the way we should go," few have the courage to argue. The experienced boss doesn't have to justify or prove his point. He just *knows*. His experience and past record of success should be enough. It would take a great deal of courage on the part of a subordinate to challenge him. Traditional organizations tend to operate on this basis.

It's quite different in a rapidly changing world, where yesterday's experience may be irrelevant or even misleading.

That is why TQManaged organizations place such a heavy emphasis on gathering and using facts and reliable, objective information to guide decision making. Goals are stated in measurable terms ("If it can't be measured, it's just a slogan"). Problems are described as objectively as possible, and charts and graphs are used to bring them into focus. Everyone who works on the problem gets the same information. Every effort is made to keep egos out of the process. Who proposes a solution is less important than why the solution makes sense and what facts back it up.

One very important side effect of decision making by fact is that it further "flattens" the organization psychologically. The person with the information is listened to more carefully than the person with the prestigious title. Everyone in the organization has a better chance to exert influence and therefore to be a part of the organization and to identify more closely with what it is doing.

WHAT STUMBLING BLOCKS SHOULD A TQMANAGER KNOW ABOUT?

Like any management approach, TQM works better in some places than others and immediately feels right to some people and wrong to others. It has failed in many organizations; even TQManagers occasionally make mistakes! To be realistic, therefore, means to be aware of some of the places where things can go wrong. In our interviews and readings we find these to be the major stumbling blocks to be avoided:

- Overselling TQM
- Setting mediocre expectations
- Poorly or inadequately diagnosing the situation
- Failing to train

- Making continuous improvement too complex and unnatural
- Behaving inconsistently
- Failing to recognize and celebrate successes

Some other stumbling blocks are also worth keeping in mind: failure to make organized labor a partner in the pursuit of TQM, lack of clarity about why the organization is going in a particular direction, mixed signals from top management, failure of some teams to "jell," and many others, some of which are out of your control. Next, we will briefly examine the more common problems.

Overselling TQM

It's easy to get excited about TQM; there are great stories to tell about how this approach to management has transformed some organizations. When you hear these success stories in a congenial group, it's natural to catch some of the enthusiasm. There's something very appealing about a fresh approach in a work setting that has become dull and routine. When we are enthusiastic and our colleagues or subordinates are skeptical, there's a strong temptation to oversell — to minimize the effort required, to exaggerate the benefits, and to underestimate the time required to get the system working. Even if we succeed in allaying the doubts, we pay a high price in credibility when our predictions fall short.

Setting Mediocre Expectations

This is the other side of the coin: introducing change so gradually that it almost seems like business as usual. If you ask me to increase my productivity by 10 percent, I can probably do that by simply working harder. However, if you *double* my goals, I have to reexamine my procedure and create a new one. One key objective of TQM is to encourage people to take a fresh look at the systems they are using and to develop better ones. When Motorola began its surge toward quality, they set

Four Sigma, or 621 errors per million, as their target. When they achieved that goal they reset their sights for Six Sigma, or 3.4 errors per million! They argue that even being 99.9 percent perfect is not good enough. (This level of performance would result in no electricity, water, or heat for 8.6 hours per year, two short or long landings at major airports per day, and 500 incorrect surgical operations per week!)

Poorly or Inadequately Diagnosing the Present Situation

TQM won't work everywhere and the landscape is littered with what some people euphemistically call "false starts." Since TQM is a major cultural change, the decision to go with it should be carefully considered. The most critical element, of course, is the solid commitment of top management. TQM requires vision and the confidence that an initial investment in planning and training will pay off in the long run, if not immediately. In addition to having support from the top, you will want to ask some questions about your own team: How do they react to change? How much confidence do they have in your organization's leadership? Which aspects of TQM will make the most sense to them and which will be the most puzzling or threatening? What particular competencies will they have to learn?

Failing to Train

In some organizations TQM has been launched so rapidly that the training program has been started only after people have experienced failure. If workers are expected to behave differently, they have to be trained. They have to feel comfortable with new procedures and understand their significance. We all like to feel competent and confident, on top of our jobs. It's naive to assume that even bright workers know how to solve problems systematically or function effectively in groups.

Making Continuous Improvement
Too Complex and Unnatural

Although *continuous improvement* is a new phrase in the management lexicon, in some sense it just extends a philosophy that good organizations have always followed. The elements of a continuous improvement culture already exist. TQManagers simply highlight and sharpen this process so that it has more power to shape behavior. They set measurable goals and plot their progress in meeting those goals.

Behaving Inconsistently

Most of the TQM words and concepts make sense: empowerment, quality, teamwork. But people in organizations have heard golden words before and all too often have been disillusioned. Executives sometimes use these words in speeches and newsletters to inspire the troops and glamorize what may be a drab and routine experience. In most organizations, however, those who are not executives take the words with a grain of salt and watch for actions. The slogan "walk your talk" has been popularized in the recent past. Words and deeds must match. Failing to check on whether a target has been reached, ignoring a worker's suggestion, or handling a customer's complaint in a cavalier manner—any of these will undermine confidence in the whole process. Your colleagues have to know what to expect of you if you are to be effective.

Failing to Recognize and Celebrate Successes

Few things are more discouraging than to have one of our special efforts ignored or taken for granted. If we are responsible employees we do the best job we can. We don't usually expect or demand anything more than a paycheck, but when we do get more recognition, it energizes us. It makes us feel differently about ourselves and the organization we serve. On the other hand, if we or our team succeed in solving a problem or setting a new record of productivity and the effort goes unnoticed, we think twice about putting ourselves out again. The disappointment is deepened, of course, if someone else gets the credit for what we have done. Successful TQManagers make a special point of letting their colleagues know how much they appreciate the goals that are met and the breakthroughs that are discovered. One of the best-tested principles of psychology states: "Behavior that is reinforced tends to be repeated." When people do the right thing, let them know it — and let them know how valued they are!

WHY HAS TQM BECOME SO POPULAR?

New management approaches are often greeted with a combination of hope and skepticism. As management becomes more complex, we are all looking for some system that will suddenly illuminate our confusing world and show us the way to get things under control. In the early years of the Industrial Revolution, "scientific management" offered a precise, systematic way to increase efficiency and productivity. Then "human relations" and "democratic leadership" seemed to be the approach to enlist the cooperation of workers. Management by objectives promised to ensure a better understanding between boss and subordinates and to elicit greater worker commitment to do the job right.

Now it's TQM that is in the spotlight. The executive who doesn't know about TQM is just not with it. Seminars, books, journals, and magazines keep it in front of us. It has wildly enthusiastic proponents and highly vocal critics and cynics. It is regarded by some as the only route to organizational survival and by others as just the latest fad in management.

When experienced managers tell us that they are enthusiastic about TQM, they generally cite one or more of these reasons:

- It has a proven track record in some very successful organizations.
- It combines and integrates many management approaches with which we are familiar.
- It is consistent with values we admire.

Let's examine each of these briefly.

TQM Has a Proven Track Record

The roster of companies that have adopted TQM as their mode of operation reads like a "Who's Who" of American industry—Motorola, Xerox, Corning, Cadillac, and Federal Express, to name just a few. Some of these companies began to take TQM seriously when they saw that they were losing significant market share to Japanese companies, where TQM was producing such dramatic results. The creation of the Malcolm Baldrige National Quality Award in 1987 gave further impetus to the Quality Movement. The seven Baldrige criteria for measuring the excellence of a company are widely used by thousands of organizations, even though they do not compete for the award itself.

In May 1991, the U.S. General Accounting Office undertook a study of companies using TQM. Their report, titled *Management Practices: U.S. Companies Improve Performance Through Quality Efforts*, concluded, "Companies that adopted quality management practices experienced an overall improvement in corporate performance. In nearly all cases, companies that used total quality management practices achieved better employee relations, higher productivity, greater customer satisfaction, increased market share, and improved profitability" (U.S. General Accounting Office, 1991, p. 2).

TQM Combines and Integrates
Many Management Approaches

The search for the best way to manage organizations has been going on for a long time. Much of the innovation and research has been done in the United States, which has been the major producer of management literature. Because the conceptual innovations occurred at different times, managers tended to adopt and discard them one at a time. TQM brings many of these concepts and practices together for the first time. Figure 1.1 gives an overview of the management theories and practices that have contributed to TQM.

Here's a quick reminder of what we have learned from each of these theories and practices:

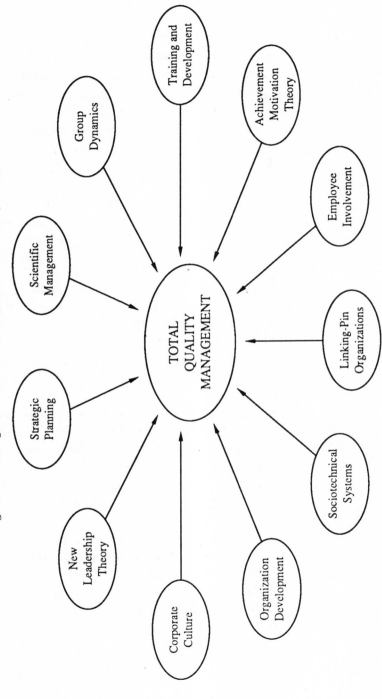

Figure 1.1. Management Theories and Practices Contributing to TQM.

- *Scientific management* taught us how to seek the best way to do a job by measuring time, motion, and results.
- *Group dynamics* taught us how to unleash the mental and emotional power of a group to solve problems.
- *Training and development* gave us insights into how people learn and showed us how to design effective learning experiences for adults.
- *Achievement motivation theory* made us aware of how much satisfaction we get from accomplishing something.
- *Employee involvement* strategies helped us to learn that workers become more responsible when they can influence the way their organization works and the way they do their jobs.
- *Linking-pin organizations,* a concept of Rensis Likert (1967), conceived of organizations as a series of overlapping teams in which each manager is a leader of one group and a member of another.
- *Sociotechnical systems* made us think of organizations as systems in which every part is interdependent with every other part.
- *Organization development* theory and practice taught us how to think about change and how to help a whole organization identify and diagnose its problems and learn to improve.
- *Corporate culture* literature made us aware of the power of beliefs and myths in influencing people to decide on their priorities and do their work.
- *New leadership theory* taught us the difference between leading and managing—and the importance of vision, trust, and empowerment in mobilizing human effort.
- *Strategic planning* gave us the technology to map an organization's environment and to plan its development in a systematic way.

An extensive body of organizational and management theory, research, and practice has emerged during the twentieth century. It has provided both the theoretical base and the technology that has made TQM possible.

Another interesting perspective on the evolution of quality is depicted in Figure 1.2. It was formulated by Bill Ginnodo, the executive director of the American Society for Quality Control. This chart reminds us that organizational interest has moved from productivity to quality to Total Quality over a period of about ten years. Following the devastation of World War II the world desperately needed to rebuild. It was natural to place the emphasis on production because there seemed to be an endless market. With the growing competition of the 1970s the emphasis shifted to quality. As competition has increased, the requirement for quality has intensified—hence Total Quality as the hallmark of the nineties and beyond.

Treatment of workers has also shifted. The Industrial Revolution, with its emphasis on mass production, viewed workers as cogs in the industrial machine. They did what

Figure 1.2. The Quality Evolution.

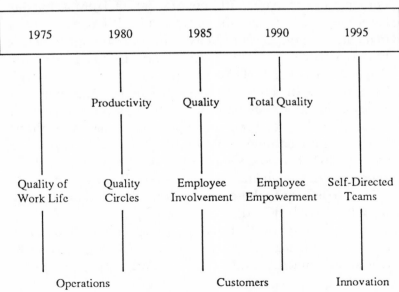

Source: Ginnodo, 1991. Used by permission.

machines could not do. As "hired hands," they were expected to perform like sophisticated machines for good wages. By the 1970s, however, more attention was given to the feelings, attitudes, and commitment of workers. People began talking about the quality of work life — and it was clear that workers were interested in more than a paycheck. Quality circles recognized the fact that workers had ideas, that they could identify and solve problems that management sometimes didn't even see. Once this was recognized, the natural next step was to involve employees more fully in the planning process itself. This continued and growing recognition of employee competence has increased until enlightened organizations today try to give employees as much power as possible to achieve agreed-upon objectives. As the responsibility and competence of employees has grown, the need for layers of managers and supervisors has decreased.

TQM Is Consistent with Values We Admire

Perhaps one of the most attractive aspects of TQM is that it is based on a very humanistic set of values. It begins with the mandate that our responsibility is to serve the customer as fully as possible. To do that, we must listen to, and understand, the customer's needs. TQM then encourages us to work collaboratively with others — to be good team members. It asks us to set goals and systematically assess our progress toward them, and then to keep on improving! It also transforms problems into learning opportunities. Who can quarrel with any of this? It almost seems as if TQM demands that we behave on the job in an idealistic fashion. We may not always be able to live up to these expectations, but it's hard to argue with them. We believe that these underlying values and beliefs are part of the power that makes TQM so attractive to many executives, managers, and workers. You can argue about its realism and practicality, but you can't argue with its guiding values!

WHY DOES TQM ONLY SUCCEED IN SOME ORGANIZATIONS?

TQM does not come with a guarantee. The Malcolm Baldrige National Quality Award for private sector companies and the President's Quality and Productivity Improvement Award for federal agencies identify some of the outstanding successes. There are also places where TQM efforts have fallen short of expectations and been abandoned. What factors seem to make the difference? We have dealt with some of them in our previous discussion of stumbling blocks. Here we would like to discuss briefly the key factors that determine the success of a TQManaged organization:

- The solid, continuing support and commitment of top management
- Careful analysis and planning
- A steering group to manage the process of change without becoming another bureaucracy

Support and Commitment of Top Management

This is an essential condition for TQM success. TQM is a major strategic process that must come from the top of the organization. Before people in the middle or at the bottom can be convinced to change, they have to be certain that this is a serious reformation. It is not the kind of program that the CEO can launch with a single speech and then delegate to an underling, while concentrating on the rest of the organization's business. Senior managers who have risen in the organization because of their particular style of management are not likely to abandon that style unless the top person makes it absolutely clear that TQM is to be the defining guideline. Where this support from the top is lacking or perceived to be only token, the effort is likely to fail.

Careful Analysis and Planning

Even if top management is committed to TQM, they will want to do a careful job of assessing the organization's readiness to accept and embrace it. In our earlier book, *The Race Without a Finish Line* (1992), we discussed at some length the questions that top management should ask themselves before launching the TQM venture. They should begin with very basic questions: What are our values? What is our mission? Who are our customers? Who are the stakeholders in our organization, the people who are affected by what we do and who have an impact upon us? What are our strengths and weaknesses? Who are our competitors? What kind of organization do we want to become? Careful, thoughtful preparation will significantly increase the chances of building a Total Quality organization.

A Steering Group to Manage Change

Successful TQM change efforts involve a team of top executives in planning and guidance. The existence of such a steering group will reassure people throughout the organization that this is not just another program, but a serious permanent change of direction. It will also be the best vehicle for assessing the pace of the change effort and deciding what resources can be devoted to it. With this kind of steady guidance, the chances for successful organizational change are significantly increased.

SUMMARY COMMENTS

In most organizations, TQM represents a major cultural change—a change in the way the organization defines itself, its priorities and values, and the way it deals with its personnel, its customers, and its suppliers. It is an organizational way of life that has become increasingly popular—and controversial—in the United States during the past few years. It embraces many long-standing management concepts and strategies, which in combination produce a very different way of operating an organization. TQM is now a buzzword or cliché in management literature. It has worked in some organizations and failed in others. Don Mizaur, director of the Federal Quality Institute (and formerly of Motorola), put the TQM movement in perspective in *Federal Quality News* (Mizaur, 1992, p. 2):

> [Quality management] has certainly grown in this country in the last decade: first business, facing economic catastrophe in a world market, followed (though less urgently) by government having to deal with declining dollars and testy taxpayers. . . . During this time lots of organizations jumped on the bandwagon labeled quality; it was the thing to do. However, some gave lip service, but not the long-term commitment. Many of them just didn't get it. . . . Quality management will survive, both in business and in government . . . because traditional management — which served us so well for so many years — isn't producing satisfactory results anymore. It isn't working because the world has changed, and it's going to keep changing, faster and faster.

We'll pick up on this perspective in the next chapter.

2

Recognizing the Challenges

Change is always a challenge, bringing elements of hope and fear. Change in the workplace—particularly when it affects our behavior—is often threatening. We have developed our approach to people, to problems, and to ideas over many years. When we find a style that feels comfortable we like to stay with it. We've seen it work and the results are predictable. When we are asked—or ordered—to change our behavior, it's only natural to feel threatened and defensive. "What's wrong with the way I'm doing my job? It's been working for me all these years. How do I know that what you're proposing will work, and that I can do it?"

THE CHALLENGE THAT STIMULATED THE QUALITY MOVEMENT

American executives and managers have had to face the challenge of change in increasing numbers since the late 1970s. Prior to that time, America was clearly the world leader in productivity. An analysis by the Massachusetts Institute of Technology Commission on Productivity (Dertouzes, 1989) found that following World War II, "American workers were more skilled on the average than those in other countries" and "American managers were the best in the world." Then the rest of the world, led by Japan, began to catch up. Quality replaced productivity as the key to commercial success in an increasingly competitive global economy. As American boards of directors and executives watched their market share decline, they began to look for reasons, ranging from high labor costs to government policies. Then a brash engineer, W. Edwards Deming (1986), documented his opinion that 85 percent of all the quality problems in American industry are the fault of management. Since he had had such a significant influence in stimulating Japanese quality efforts, his statement could not be ignored.

As American managers listened to Deming and other quality leaders like Philip B. Crosby (1979), Joseph M. Juran (1989), and Armand V. Feigenbaum (1956), they began to reexamine their assumptions and practices. Even U.S. military organizations began to change. (In fact, it was a U.S. Navy psychologist, Nancy Warren, who first suggested the name Total Quality Management, which was adopted as the label for this new approach to organizing and managing.) Governmental agencies at local, state, and federal levels have joined the move toward TQM. The Federal Quality Institute was established in 1988 to introduce senior officials in the federal government to TQM and to be the primary source of information, training, and consulting service for federal agencies. In 1987 the U.S. Congress created the Baldrige National Quality Award to encourage excellence in all aspects of business management. In 1989 a comparable award—the President's Quality and Productivity Improvement Award—was created to recognize excellence in the overall management and customer service of federal agencies. Even educational institutions—from grammar schools to universities—have begun to change their mode of managing.

Learning to survive and prosper in the Information Age

presents a number of challenges to organizational leaders and individual managers. Some say that the "Third Industrial Revolution" is under way (Deming, 1986), a revolution that requires a new approach to management. As Lester Thurow writes in his provocative book, *Head to Head: The Coming Battle Among Japan, Europe and America* (1992), "Beliefs about the *right* management style change very slowly and only under great duress" (p. 272). The rapid movement of events, however, requires that American managers reexamine their style immediately and make the necessary changes while there is still time. We believe that the subtitle of the 1988 book by C. Jackson Grayson and Carla O'Dell, *American Business: A Two-Minute Warning*, does not exaggerate the urgency of change.

Let's look at the major challenges that now face the TQManager. Some of these may fit what you now believe and are already doing. Others may require you to reexamine some of the assumptions that guide your behavior. Still others may suggest whole new approaches to your job. Based on our survey of successful TQManagers, we consider these twelve challenges to be the most important:

1. The challenge to understand all that TQM involves
2. The challenge to be a good supplier to your customers
3. The challenge to be a good customer
4. The challenge to be a good coach
5. The challenge to be a team leader
6. The challenge to be a good team member
7. The challenge to be a process observer
8. The challenge to be a planner and problem solver
9. The challenge to improve
10. The challenge to be a good communicator
11. The challenge to be a good listener
12. The challenge to keep learning

Let's discuss each of these challenges as a prelude to Part Two of this book, which helps you in applying TQM.

THE CHALLENGE TO UNDERSTAND ALL THAT TQM INVOLVES

Many managers don't take the time to understand TQM before making up their minds about it. Since TQM builds on many past theories and practices, managers may develop what psychologists call a "false feeling of familiarity" and accept or reject it on the basis of a partial understanding. It's like standing in some small town you have never visited before and thinking, "I *must* have been here," because your eye has caught familiar landmarks like the firehouse, the church, and the drugstore all in the "right" places. Managers hear familiar phrases — employee involvement, empowerment, teams, measurement — and they conclude that this is the same old stuff under a new label. Some managers have even told us, "We already practice teamwork; we have several quality circles." This is a very natural reaction in an age when we talk in shorthand and are expected to make quick decisions on fragmentary information.

We'd like to underscore our conviction that TQM represents a revolutionary approach to operating an organization. TQM is *not* just a new label for commonsense management. It is *not* just a composite of past theories and practices (though many are included in it). It is *not* just a new management technique or program. It *is* a different approach to conceptualizing and managing an organization — a new paradigm. Here is one case where the whole is greater than the sum of its parts. Each piece by itself may seem sensible and obvious, but taken together they represent a dramatic shift in the way an organization actually goes about its business. We urge you to examine all of the aspects of TQM carefully before you make a judgment about it. (By the time you finish this book, all of the key elements will have come into focus.)

For example, it sounds like an advertising cliché to say, "The customer comes first." But if you take that *seriously* — as TQManaged organizations do — lots of things change. The people who are closest to the customer become more powerful, because they know what the customer wants and appreciates. Priorities are assigned and quality standards are based on what the customers think.

THE CHALLENGE TO BE
A GOOD SUPPLIER
TO YOUR CUSTOMERS

The TQManaged organization is thought of as a complex system of supplier-customer relationships. Every individual and every department is expected to identify its customers and determine what those customers' needs are. Internal customers provide their internal suppliers with information about what they require to do their job most effectively. This formulation of organizational relationships has a profound effect on the amount and kind of communication that flows in the system and the kinds of relationships that develop.

If you and your team want to be good suppliers, you must first be clear about who your customers are. Who, inside or outside the organization, uses the products or services that you provide? Do you know how they use what you produce? Do you know about the time pressures they operate under, and how well you are helping them to meet their deadlines? Is your product or service given to them in a way that makes it easy to use? Do they anticipate changes in their requirements that you ought to know about? How do they rate the service you provide, and how would they like to see it improved? If quality is defined as "meeting the customer's requirements," you will want to make certain that you have the kind of relationships and communication arrangements that ensure that you are up-to-date!

THE CHALLENGE TO BE A GOOD CUSTOMER

You are also a customer. You need input from other people inside and outside the organization to keep on top of your job. Your suppliers need accurate, up-to-date information about your requirements. They need to know about your plans in time to make adjustments. They need to know how satisfied you are with the kind of help they are giving to you. They need your expressions of appreciation, as well as your suggestions for improvement. You may want them to participate in some of your planning sessions and suggest that they reciprocate. Whatever can be done to strengthen supplier-customer relationships has proved to be a boon to both quality and personal satisfaction.

THE CHALLENGE TO BE A GOOD COACH

As a manager, you are held responsible for the work your subordinates do. This is true in traditional organizations and TQManaged organizations. Managers are frustrated and irritated by subordinates who have limited talent or commitment to do the job. How should you approach this problem? Here there's a marked difference between traditional managers and TQManagers.

Traditional managers usually regard their subordinates as expendable. The manager's responsibility is to make certain that the task is clear and that the worker gets the required training. From there on the manager only checks to see whether the work is being done properly. If it's not — because

of either incompetence or unwillingness to do the job right —
the manager is expected to give adequate warnings (sometimes prescribed by union contracts) and, if they produce no
results, to arrange for transfer or dismissal of the employee. In
the process, the motivational problem is dealt with by using
the carrot-and-stick approach with varying degrees of subtlety.

TQManagers view workers as members of their team.
They feel responsible for making the task clear and providing
each team member with the training, resources, and other
support needed to do the job. They are coaches, operating on
the assumption that each worker wants to do a good job, both
for herself and for the reputation of the team. Like any good
coach, TQManagers work to keep up the morale of the team
through information, encouragement, and recognition of
work well done. They identify with their team, not just with
management. They assume — until it is proved otherwise —
that workers want to do a good job and get genuine satisfaction
from their accomplishments and from being members of a
productive team.

THE CHALLENGE TO BE
A TEAM LEADER

Although teamwork has always been applauded in most American organizations, more attention has usually been given to
individual performance. Individuals, rather than groups, are
viewed as the source of new ideas. We tend to talk in terms of
individual initiative and *individual* effort. And we rarely are
optimistic when we turn a problem over to a committee
(although it's one easy way of getting a sticky problem off our
desk!). We make jokes about group meetings and how much
time they waste. The result is often a negative, self-fulfilling
prophecy; we expect mediocre results from groups and our
planning and running of meetings produces exactly that.

TQManagers think differently about teams. They learn
how to form and manage teams so that they become in-

creasingly productive. As Thomas Kayser put it in his book, *Mining Group Gold* (1990), they move "from unstructured and individualistic problem solving to disciplined and predominantly collaborative efforts" (p. xv). This means developing the skills needed to plan, conduct, and participate in meetings. The key challenge, however, is to understand what teamwork really involves and how to create and nourish team efforts. (We discuss techniques for doing this in Chapter Seven.)

THE CHALLENGE TO BE A GOOD TEAM MEMBER

As a TQManager you will be expected to join with colleagues to form teams — teams to analyze problems, teams to solve problems, teams to plan. Often these teams will cross institutional and disciplinary lines. (For example, the most successful companies have found that by forming teams of designers, engineers, and production experts who plan together, they can reduce significantly the time required to get a new product to market.) To be a good member of such a team — or any team — involves developing the ability to learn from colleagues, to express your ideas clearly, to maintain an atmosphere of cooperation and mutual respect, and to regard differences of opinion as opportunities for mutual growth.

The TQManaged organization differs from those American companies in which competitiveness is a highly valued mode of operation. The spirit of competition often energizes and spurs individuals, departments, and divisions to do their best. When people want to win they try harder. Who would not want to be the best manager or a member of the best department? In sports, most records are set in competitive situations. In an organization, it's important to be clear about who your competitor is. If it's another organization, a competitive spirit may indeed spur you to work smarter, harder, and with greater teamwork. Unfortunately, the competitive spirit often moves inside the organization and people who should be teammates feel and behave like rivals. The goal is transformed from an effort to be the best into a fight to win at all costs and to defeat your internal rivals. When this happens, energies are diverted, collaboration diminishes, and the output of the organization suffers. Most of us have seen such situations, where colleagues get caught up in internal struggles that sap the energy and attention of whole groups of people.

Effective TQManagers appreciate the value of a spirited effort to do one's best and to exchange competing ideas and plans. However, they also recognize the overriding need to function as a team in order to accomplish the goals to which everyone is committed.

THE CHALLENGE TO BE A PROCESS OBSERVER

Traditional managers often pride themselves on being result-oriented. They say that it's the bottom line that really counts; how results are obtained is of secondary interest. While this sounds like a sensible, realistic approach, in reality it can be very costly. It's the kind of thinking that sometimes leads managers to take shortcuts to meet a monthly quota. It encourages executives to do short-range planning, delaying some expenditures so that the next quarterly financial report will be on target. It's also the kind of costly strategy that requires an inspection at the end of a production line to catch defective products before they are shipped to the customer.

TQManagers, on the other hand, give their major attention to the *process* by which their organization creates products or services. Their assumption is that a perfect process will produce a perfect product every time, and that's their goal. Defects in the product or service simply reflect defects in the system that created them. So when a defect occurs, the TQManager and her team examine the system that created it to find the flaw. When that flaw is found and corrected, the defect will disappear.

THE CHALLENGE TO BE A PLANNER AND PROBLEM SOLVER

In a turbulent time, planning never stops. Peter Vaill (1989) describes ours as a "white water society" in which there is constant turbulence. To survive, we must continually review what's happening in the part of the world with which we interact and decide how best to direct our energies. No longer does this happen only at the executive level in healthy organizations. Often the people closest to the customer see the problems first. TQManagers, therefore, need to hone their planning and problem-solving skills to help keep their organization healthy. This often includes learning from dysfunctions that they spot or mistakes that are made.

Almost every organizational expert will tell you that traditional organizations discourage creativity by the way they react to mistakes. When a significant error occurs, one of the first reactions is to ask, "Who is responsible?" The individual or group that is identified can usually expect some kind of punishment, ranging from subtle expressions of criticism to dismissal from the organization. Where errors are dealt with in this manner, managers and employees quickly learn to be cautious. They take fewer risks and go to great lengths to avoid taking responsibility. They spend a great deal of time documenting what they do so that their records will back them up if something goes wrong. The cost to the organization, of course, is a loss of creativity by managers and workers. The safest way to survive in an organization where the practice is to fix blame is to hunker down and do what you're told to do. Why take chances by trying something new? If it's successful you *may* get some credit, but if it fails, you *know* you'll be called to account.

TQManaged organizations develop a very different climate. TQManagers are expected to encourage experimentation and take risks. Mistakes are viewed as occasions for inspecting the process more carefully. The important question is not "Who is responsible?" but "What part of the process caused this to happen and how can we fix it?" If it's a significant error, it may warrant creation of a team to take hold of the problem, analyze it, and propose a solution. The result is freedom from the fear of making a mistake, which in turn relieves everyone of the need to look over his shoulder, document every movement, and live in a generally defensive way. A key responsibility of the TQManager is to communicate and practice this approach to problems.

THE CHALLENGE TO IMPROVE

One of the principal contributions the Japanese have made to management theory is the concept and practice of *Kaizen* (pronounced Ký-zen). Massaki Imai (1986) called it "the key to Japan's competitive success." It is the commitment to work toward steady, continual improvement. This does not always feel comfortable to Americans. We tend to appreciate short, intensive bursts of activity, followed by periods of relaxation. We look for and celebrate breakthroughs rather than less dramatic, incremental changes.

We frequently overlook small defects in a process, as long as things are working. By contrast, the Japanese have demonstrated clearly the power of *Kaizen* — the day-by-day, week-by-week discovery of small steps that make the process more efficient, economical, and dependable. Developing this point of view is critical to the success of the TQManager. The quest for a better way to do things never stops. When David Kearns was president of Xerox, he talked about "a race without a finish line." We liked that phrase so much that we made it the title of our first book on TQM! (Schmidt and Finnigan, 1992).

THE CHALLENGE TO BE
A GOOD COMMUNICATOR

Although communication has always been a key requirement of good management (and will appear on any list of managers' key concerns), it is even more important in the TQManaged organization. If every member of the team is to pursue the same goals, they all have to be kept informed. If they are to get excited about achieving objectives, they have to know how much progress is being made. If they have to keep improving their performance, they have to get continual feedback.

TQManaged organizations depend on communication that flows in all directions: up, down, and laterally. The TQManager has to monitor the process, spot flaws in it, and improve it. Internal and external customers have to let suppliers know what they need. Suppliers have to let their customers know what they can realistically provide. Communication is, indeed, the lifeblood of the organization. By constantly improving their own communication skills and helping their colleagues to do the same, TQManagers add significantly to the vitality of the organization.

THE CHALLENGE TO BE
A GOOD LISTENER

Communication is always two-sided: telling and listening. We usually pay more attention to the former than to the latter, since listening is often thought of as a passive activity. There is considerable evidence that most managers are poor listeners, particularly to subordinates and people from other parts of the organization. We won't go into all of the dimensions of "active listening" here, but we did want to make certain that it is on the TQManager's list of necessary competencies.

THE CHALLENGE
TO KEEP LEARNING

There was a time in traditional organizations when workers or managers who had proven their competence and loyalty to the organization could count on job security and fairly regular promotion. In a reasonably stable environment, seniority usually meant that the more experienced persons knew how the system operated and were the most valuable members of the organizational family. Those who wanted to rise more quickly could take outside classes on their own, but it wasn't essential to keep their job or get periodic raises and promotions.

TQManagers know that the ground rules are very different now. In his book, *The Fifth Discipline*, Peter Senge (1990) uses the subtitle *The Art and Practice of the Learning Organization*. He makes the point that "the organizations that will truly excel in the future will be the organizations that discover how to tap people's commitment and capacity to learn at *all* levels in an organization" (p. 4). The one certain thing about your organization's future activity is that it will be different from what it is now. It will be vulnerable to competing organizations that learn more quickly and are more creative, and those organizations may exist in almost any part of the world. We discuss the learning organization more fully in Chapter Seven, but the nature of the TQManager's choice is captured below.

On Choosing to Learn

It was written in ancient times:
　　"*For everything there is a season and a time for every matter*
　　　under heaven . . . a time to be born and time to die . . .
　　　　a time to sow and a time to reap . . ."

When life is at its best we have the freedom to choose:

There is a time to *plan* and a time to *act*
　　and in between, *if we choose*, there is also a time to
　　examine the assumptions that underlie our plans and
　　the forces that affect our actions.

There is a time to *talk* and a time to *listen*
and in between, *if we choose,* there is a time to learn
how human beings come to understand one another.

There is a time to *organize* and a time to *act alone*
and in between, *if we choose,* there is a time to
understand how people link their wills and energies to
reach a common goal.

There is a time to *lead* and a time to *follow*
and in between, *if we choose,* there is a time to discover
what makes us want to do the will of another.

There is a time to be *firm* in our control of others and a
time to let our grip be *loose*
and in between, *if we choose,* there is a time to know
more fully the power and risks of freedom.

There is a time to *support* and a time to *confront*
and in between, *if we choose,* there is a time to reflect on
how we can help others to do their best.

And so it goes in every arena of our lives, as we initiate or
respond, decide or act.

Each experience takes a moment of our time, and
whether it passes unused or becomes a text for our
learning
is up to us — *for only we can choose!*

W.H.S.
1965

PART TWO

MASTERING THE FIVE KEY TQMANAGERIAL COMPETENCIES

TQM rests upon a genuine, hands-on commitment from an organization's managers. It is their behavior and actions that provide the leadership for Total Quality. This leadership and commitment do not happen because they say it will, but because they "walk their talk."

TQManagers know that Total Quality does not change their traditional management responsibilities and accountability. Decision making still belongs to the TQManager, as do planning, organizing, communicating, and evaluating performance. What *does* change, however, is the manager's capacity as a teacher and team leader, which is enlivened and expanded. TQManagers "partner" with their employees to establish work processes that are consistent with the principles and guidelines of TQM.

In this part we will look at the manager's new role by examining the five key competencies a manager must master to succeed in a TQM organization and become an effective TQManager. These competencies are

1. Developing relationships of openness and trust

2. Building collaboration and teamwork

45

3.   Managing by fact

4.   Supporting results through recognition and rewards

5.   Creating a learning and continuously improving
     organization

3

One:
Developing Relationships
of Openness and Trust

Many managers have found that their single most power-ful management tool is trust. When their subordinates, col-leagues, and boss trust them, things work smoothly. They can take risks. They can say what they think and admit their mistakes. They can deal forthrightly with those around them. And they can feel sure that they will be told the truth, even when it is unpleasant. This is the kind of trust that can only blossom in an environment of openness.

Openness and trust are the brick and mortar of Total Quality—without them there is no solid base on which a manager can engage employees in the pursuit of continuous improvement. As any manager knows, the easy part is under-standing what openness and trust are; putting them to work is significantly more difficult. This chapter is designed to help you master the art of openness and trust.

REFLECTIONS ON
OPENNESS AND TRUST

When trust is low or nonexistent, everything becomes more complicated. Communication is less open. People take fewer risks and admit fewer mistakes. They spend their time protecting themselves from blame, writing memos to explain their actions. How does a TQManager go about developing openness and trust? To get the most out of this chapter, we suggest that you first take a few minutes to do some personal reflecting, using Exhibit 3.1.

THE RELEVANCE OF OPENNESS AND TRUST

Openness is the willingness to advocate what you believe is right without fear of the consequences. It is characterized by risk taking and begins with your personal attitude and frankness. *Trust*, on the other hand, is conditioned by the behaviors of others and requires reliance on the integrity, ability, and character of other people. It is based on the confident belief and faith that people say what they mean and will do what they say. This kind of openness breeds trust. It begins at the top of an organization, cascades downward, spreads across, and fills the organization with a sense of common purpose, without sacrificing the value of diverse opinions.

The energy that initiates and builds openness and trust is communication. It *starts* when a manager gives people the information they need to understand the organization's goals and how their own job supports those goals. It *expands* when a manager makes sure that employees have the knowledge and skills they need to do their jobs. And it *continues* when a manager solicits employees' ideas and feedback on how the whole process can be improved. (This is the step that many managers find hardest to take.)

Many managers have trouble fully trusting their employees. They usually have risen in their organizations because they were willing and able to take responsibility. When future success is dependent upon what other people decide and do, they become anxious. It is not surprising that many new managers want to keep control firmly in their own hands. It is

Exhibit 3.1. Reflections on Openness and Trust.

1. Think of a boss you trusted (either one you have now or had in the past) and three things this boss did that helped you decide that he was trustworthy:

   ■ _____

   ■ _____

   ■ _____

2. Check your own behavior. How often is each of these statements true of you?

Note: Some of these statements can be regarded as positive, others as negative.	Almost Never	Rarely	Sometimes	Frequently	Almost Always
■ I consider that keeping my work group and colleagues fully informed is a top priority.	—	—	—	—	—
■ I work at demonstrating confidence in my work group.	—	—	—	—	—
■ I like to take risks with those around me.	—	—	—	—	—
■ I try to make it comfortable for people to give me their honest feedback on how they view my actions.	—	—	—	—	—
■ I am a good listener and learn from what I hear.	—	—	—	—	—
■ I enjoy telling my subordinates what to do, especially when I know more than they do.	—	—	—	—	—
■ I can be very critical when someone makes a serious mistake, whether it was intentional or not.	—	—	—	—	—
■ When someone brings me information that I don't like, I let them know it.	—	—	—	—	—
■ I hold people accountable when they support positions with which I disagree.	—	—	—	—	—
■ I feel uncomfortable when someone tries to get me to change.	—	—	—	—	—

After you have finished reading this chapter, return to this chart, review your responses, and make notes on how you might want to change.

natural for them to assume that their subordinates do not feel the same level of commitment to the job that they do. But TQManagers start with a different set of assumptions.

First, TQManagers see their employees as a work group—a team, of which they are also a part. Second, they believe that their team *wants* to do a good job and will get a sense of satisfaction from achieving clearly defined goals. Sterling Livingston's research on the Pygmalion effect makes it clear that when managers communicate this kind of trust and confidence they increase the probability that employees will do their best (Livingston, 1969). Deming (1986, p. 24) puts it simply: "Remove barriers that rob people of pride of workmanship."

Managers who are freed from the anxiety of constantly checking on their team are able to focus on a different set of issues: "How can I help my team members get the resources they need to do their job?" "How can I make the work environment more conducive to healthy work?" "How can we improve the process by which we add value to the material we receive from our suppliers?" "What can we learn from the problems that occur?" When openness and trust mark the work climate, managers find that problems surface more quickly and clearly. Solutions to these problems may take longer to develop, but usually they correct the problem permanently. What follows is the continuous improvement of work processes and productivity.

What do TQManagers do with team members who can't handle responsibility? They confront them with their performance goals, the record, and the discrepancies. The question then becomes: "What caused this, and what can *we* do about it?" It becomes a problem to be solved. If it is clear that an employee either cannot, or does not want to, change his behavior to achieve the required goal, he must be removed from that job. TQManagers trust people and try to give optimal opportunity and support, but they also recognize that the decision to accept responsibility ultimately lies with each individual.

TQManagers know that this kind of openness and trust

starts with their own honesty and openness. It is a *quid pro quo* that always begins with the manager, because it is only after a manager has demonstrated her willingness to operate in such an environment that reciprocation will follow. Before employees can be expected to take risks they need to know that their manager will lead by cultivating this new relationship; therefore, TQM can only flourish when a manager's personal style is one of openness, trust, and honest appraisal.

A manager who wants to adopt the personal practices that lead to openness and trust must first focus on those few vital behaviors that will best help to achieve this goal. At the same time he will have to be aware of the behaviors that can block his progress. These behaviors are outlined in Figure 3.1.

HELPING FACTORS: FIVE THINGS THE TQMANAGER CAN DO

Communicate Clearly and Consistently

Success in using TQM depends on consistent and credible communication in the broadest sense of the word. When regular communication is practiced by a manager, it opens pathways for observing and learning about the development of openness and trust. TQManagers know that people work more productively when they have relevant information about their company and its goals, know their jobs and performance goals, and know what they can do to help shape their organization's future. People prefer to receive this kind of information from their immediate manager and they want to know from their manager that their efforts are appreciated. That is why TQManagers *listen* to their employees; *respect* their employees, both as persons and as workers; *encourage* their employees to higher levels of performance by positive reinforcement; and *provide guidance and direction* to their employees when necessary.

Figure 3.1. Building Openness and Trust.

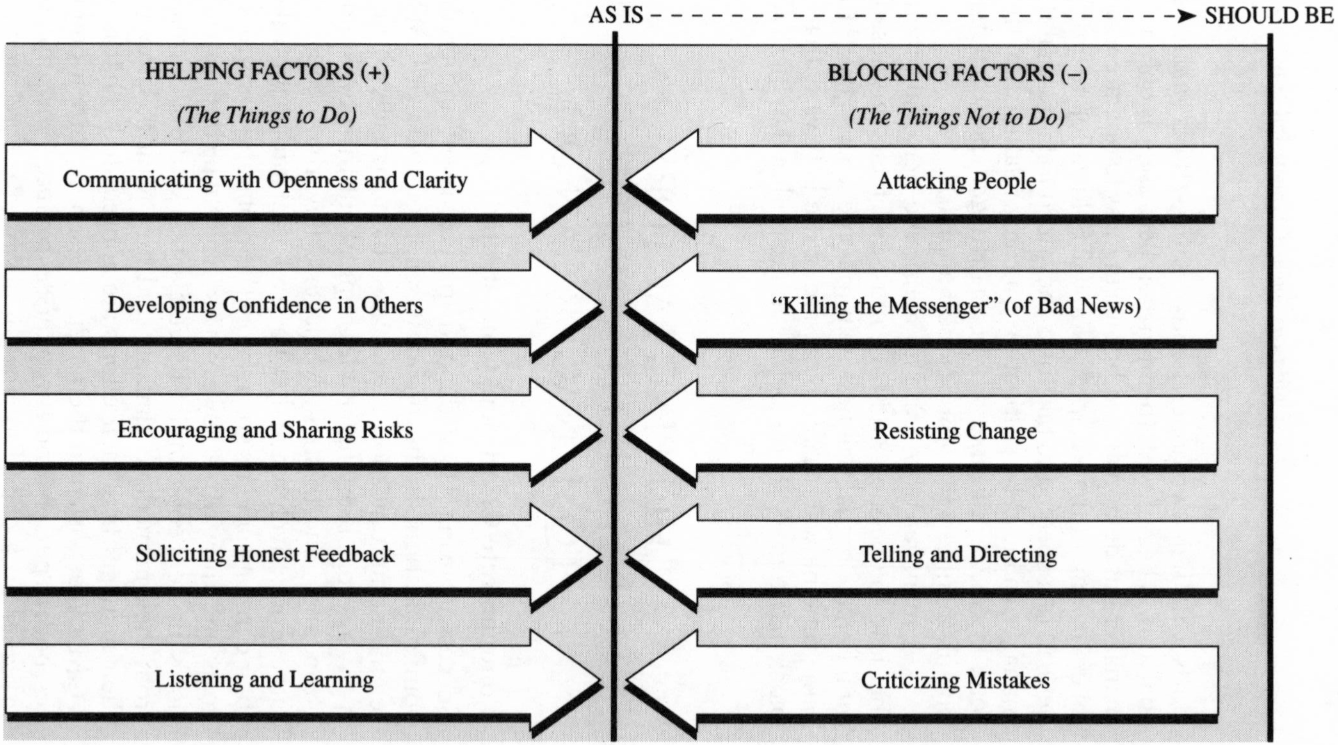

AS IS -▶ SHOULD BE

BLOCKING FACTORS (−)
(The Things Not to Do)

Attacking People

"Killing the Messenger" (of Bad News)

Resisting Change

Telling and Directing

Criticizing Mistakes

HELPING FACTORS (+)
(The Things to Do)

Communicating with Openness and Clarity

Developing Confidence in Others

Encouraging and Sharing Risks

Soliciting Honest Feedback

Listening and Learning

TQManagers conduct two-way communication with their employees in as many ways as possible, including round-table meetings with the whole team or subgroups and one-on-one sessions with individuals, but especially by just "walking around." TQManagers know the importance of spending time in their employees' work area, observing, listening, and soliciting feedback on a regular basis. The TQManager wants to be certain that senior management's policy decisions reach her people quickly. She wants to be certain that her employees know how these decisions will affect their work. And she wants to be certain that management learns how effective their decisions are by knowing what is happening locally. For these reasons the TQManager does the following:

- Communicates the organization's business goals and accomplishments on a regular basis and shares the success stories of other teams

- Engages with work groups in problem solving and collaborative decision making, so that they can obtain for their team whatever knowledge or data they require

- "Inspects" the team's work processes and accomplishments and keeps a close eye on what the team needs to improve performance

- Adopts some kind of feedback tool and process to learn how her management style is affecting her employees

- Surveys employees' attitudes regarding the organization, including their work, pay, benefits, and progress toward Total Quality

Develop the Self-Confidence of Others

The level and depth of confidence of a manager's employees and colleagues will largely determine the extent to which openness and trust will be allowed to operate in the organization. Confidence does not just happen. It requires a manager's serious effort to develop with the people around him the kind of self-esteem and knowledge that breed confidence. TQManagers focus on building this kind of confidence in their employees by meeting their individual needs for self-respect, personal improvement, and professional development. They know that by providing their people with positive feedback, diligently avoiding personal attacks, and painstakingly making certain that their people know everything they need to know in order to be successful at their job, they are helping to create a team of confident individuals.

Employee confidence is also important to TQManagers because employees are better able to improve the work *system* than they can themselves, and most problems are with the work system, not with the workers. TQManagers know that people will support what they themselves have created, so they try to ensure that their employees have input into the decisions that affect their work. They also know that employees speak more freely when they believe that managers can be influenced to make changes. Not only does this promote openness and trust, but it also builds teamwork and fosters commitment to continuous performance improvement. With increased confidence in her team, a TQManager can expect to see some striking changes:

- Employees taking ownership of their jobs
- Employees showing a deeper commitment to the organization's goals
- Employees working at improving their competence with the tools and processes of Total Quality

A team of such employees values openness and trust. For that reason they are encouraged to state their needs aloud because that is "the way we do things around here." In turn, they are stimulated to learn more about their jobs and this makes them more responsible. As employee confidence grows, it fosters opportunities for feedback for both the employee and the manager, which provides the team members with greater accessibility to their primary resource for information, tools, and help—their TQManager. It is when these dynamics are at work that the TQManager sees the real return for his new management style!

Encourage and Share Risks

Openness and trust are synonymous with sharing risks, and risk taking can be thought of as publicly supporting what you think is right. Risk taking enables individuals and organizations to overcome the barriers to creative thinking and problem solving and makes possible the breakthroughs that lead to competitive advantage. Alexander Graham Bell was once asked how he handled the disappointment of his twenty thousand failed experiments before he successfully invented the telephone. He replied that he thought of them not as failures, but as the discovery of twenty thousand ways that would not work. Like Alexander Graham Bell, organizations that learn from their mistakes are able to recognize failures without negative effects. Managers who want their employees to propose and discuss ideas not only must believe this, but also must be willing to take risks themselves. "CYA" may have been a successful style in the past, but it will not work in TQManagement. A manager has to allow her employees to learn from their mistakes. If she punishes mistakes, no one will plow new ground.

TQManagers also know that risk taking is not a *laissez-faire* attitude. Risks are only taken after thoughtful examination and expression of ideas and data. In his book, *Innovations and Entrepreneurship,* Peter Drucker (1985, p. 139) related a personal experience that is worth repeating here. He wrote:

> A year ago I attended a university symposium on entrepreneurship at which a number of psychologists spoke. Although their papers disagreed on everything else, they all talked of an "entrepreneurial personality," which was characterized by a "propensity for risk-taking." A well known and successful innovator and entrepreneur who had built a process-based innovation into a substantial worldwide business in the space of twenty-five years was then asked to comment. He said: "I find myself baffled by

your papers. I think I know as many successful innovators and entrepreneurs as anyone, beginning with myself. I have never come across an 'entrepreneurial personality.' The successful ones I know all have, however, one thing—and only one thing—in common: they are not 'risk-takers.' They try to define the risks they have to take and to minimize them as much as possible. Otherwise none of us could have succeeded." This jibes with my own experience. . . . The innovators I know are successful to the extent to which they define risks and confine them. They are successful to the extent to which they systematically analyze the sources of innovative opportunity, then pinpoint the opportunity and exploit it.

TQManagers are managers who practice the principles of quality day in and day out, thoroughly understand and have complete ownership of quality concepts and tools, and possess the skills to take those concepts into action. They know that it is much easier for employees to take a chance on changing a process for quality's sake in an organization committed to Total Quality than in one where the first rule is "Don't rock the boat."

TQManagers also know that some people are reluctant by nature to take risks and will require personal support and encouragement. They are also conscious of the fact that attitudes and reward systems may discourage taking risks, so they strive to establish reward systems that support risk taking. This is why TQManagers advocate the changes in the organization that are necessary to foster, applaud, and recognize risk taking to improve work processes and meet customer requirements.

Solicit Honest Feedback

Nothing will reinforce a manager's commitment to openness and trust more quickly than the continuous monitoring of his own behavior from the feedback of his employees. In his book, *Beyond Ambition*, Robert Kaplan (1991) quotes an executive who talked about "the constructive critics who care enough about the organization and the person to help him and tell that person how his behavior is impacting on the organization" (p. 37). As the author notes, the critical factor is the manager himself. Will he be willing to have his behavior and motives characterized or criticized? In this regard TQManagers take these three steps:

1.   They do not isolate themselves from others on the team.

2.   They do not assume the team knows where they stand.

3.   They select a method or tool for obtaining employee feedback.

The feedback tools that we believe help best are those that measure management style and are tied directly to TQM behaviors. Some devices that can be used are employee surveys, employee focus groups, and third-party interviews, as well as the organization's customary communication channels such as employee access to their manager's manager and suggestion systems. Good TQManagers regularly solicit feedback on employees' attitudes and their satisfaction with the organization's quality effort and management processes. This is done either as part of a management style survey or by some other instrument. (One example of such an instrument is given in Chapter Eight.)

Feedback on the effectiveness of the organization's transition to TQM is also important. Too often senior management orders changes they presume will be carried out, only to discover later that the direction has been ignored. It is important for TQManagers to develop multiple, redundant, and sensitive mechanisms for gathering feedback about the transition to TQM. By using this feedback to develop actions that adjust her management style, a TQManager demonstrates openness to change her behavior and trust in her employees' help. This willingness to be open to criticism and to develop personal action plans for change is a powerful signal that says, "I want to make things better for us all."

Listen and Learn

Most breakthroughs in work activity are the result of insights gained from personal experience. It behooves an organization to facilitate the transmission of such knowledge to as many workers as possible in the shortest time possible. But this process doesn't work if the manager is not "listening" to his team—to their ideas, their problems, and their experiences.

We learn from successful quality organizations that people must *know* that they are listened to, that their ideas are considered and have some impact. When this doesn't happen, employees keep their ideas to themselves. Teamwork works when TQManagers provide feedback on ideas and ways to implement the best suggestions. Teams quickly die, or become a waste of time, when nobody takes their recommendations seriously. TQManagers can tell when they are listening, because they are immersed in a flood of new ideas.

BLOCKING FACTORS: FIVE THINGS THE TQMANAGER SHOULD NOT DO

Don't Attack People—Attack Problems

A manager's ability to initiate an open and trusting environment is in direct proportion to how effectively she reduces the amount of stress in volatile issues and is fair to everyone involved. Personal labeling raises defensiveness and provides the ingredients for an emotional explosion. By keeping the focus on issues and on the steps that are necessary for corrective action, the TQManager avoids holding employees responsible for the negative effects of the issue at hand. Without this freedom, teams will not share their knowledge regarding problems. Managers know that when a problem occurs it is no time for hidden agendas; it is a time for honestly stating the facts so the group can get off to a good start in attacking the issue. Employees must be able to supply information without believing that they have to interpret it for better reception or suggest how the information should be used in order to avoid conflict. It is a wise TQManager who zeros in on correcting negative *behaviors* without labeling or classifying *people*.

Don't "Kill the Messenger"

Managers who "kill the messenger" of bad news not only stifle TQM; they blindfold themselves. As a CEO observed, "People have to be sure they're being asked honestly, and that what they are going to get back is not a Louisville Slugger" (Kaplan, 1991, p. 38). It only takes one employee whose bad news is met this way to alert the rest of the team that they should take their ball and go home. When that happens, problems do not surface, resource needs go unaddressed, and CYA becomes the paramount style of the team. Rather than management by fact, hope and rationalization become the day-to-day process. The manager can only wait until one of those camouflaged problems slips past him and he will be on the receiving end of a Louisville Slugger.

By treating errors and problems as opportunities for learning, rather than mistakes to be punished, TQManagers eliminate the need to "kill the messenger." They know that most people are tired of being bearers of bad news in organizations where mistakes are regularly punished and that turning things around will not be easy. It takes encouragement and "walking the talk." It is not uncommon to hear a manager tell an employee, "Don't bring me problems, bring me solutions." This can be shortsighted. Employees usually solve problems if they can, but many problems are beyond their abilities, resources, or authority. A TQManager looks for problems, and once they are identified, she helps employees uncover solutions.

Don't Resist Change

Past experience is valuable, but habits can also prevent us from looking at things in new ways. Many people stick to old ways of doing things even when new approaches can be very productive and satisfying, simply because they are comfortable with the tried-and-true. If we do not monitor or evaluate the solutions to problems we implement, we may fail to recognize that changing conditions or just the passing of time has nullified our solution. When that happens, we say, "See, it doesn't do any good to change the system. Let's save ourselves all the time, money, and aggravation and make do with the way things are." It is our nature to resist changes to things that are familiar and comfortable. When we *do* buy in to change, we want it to be quick, dramatic, and painless—a Gulf War rather than a Vietnam. Many would argue that it is easier and safer to keep things as they are than to learn openness and trust.

Opening people's minds to new ideas usually produces conflict because old cultures, habits, ideas, and practices seldom shift without some irritation. Often, the organization in which there is no irritation or conflict is one that is not changing or growing. It is probably an organization in trouble. In general, people will support a change if (1) they are convinced that the present situation is not desirable, (2) the proposed "future" is clear, (3) the path toward that future is clear and realistic, and (4) the cost of the change is not too high. A TQManager can overcome resistance to change by helping his people understand the answers to four questions:

1. How will we be affected by the change? (What will we gain and what will we lose?)

2. What are the advantages of the changed condition?

3. How bad or unacceptable is the current condition?

4. How ready are we to take the first steps to bring about the necessary changes?

Don't Tell and Direct

Good communication is a prerequisite for openness and trust. TQManagers communicate regularly, frequently, and candidly. They provide their teams with the business information necessary to solve work-related problems, and they direct them to the problem-solving opportunities with the greatest return. Because the TQManager delegates real authority to her team, it is essential that she define the parameters and constraints for the team's work. When she "orders" the team to do something and tells them precisely how to do it, the manager is limiting them to predetermined solutions. This is the opposite of openness and trust. As managers we have been taught to "tell" and to "direct," and most of us are pretty good at it. But we have to remember that good management in a TQM organization is the same as good management in any well-operated organization: it is neither autocratic nor laissez-faire. Instead, it is a management style committed to the principles of empowerment and responsive to the capacity and needs of the team, not of the manager. Rather than "telling and directing," the TQManager demands excellence but trusts in the willingness of the team members to do the right things, and to do things right.

Don't Criticize Mistakes

One of the most important tasks of any manager is to manage human performance. It also may be the most difficult thing a manager has to do. Evaluating another person's performance is a particularly difficult and sensitive responsibility. Employees need feedback on their mistakes in order to resume good performance and improve standards, but too much criticism can cause some individuals and teams to take low profiles. When that happens they avoid new ground and limit their efforts to the tasks that they are confident they can do successfully.

When a TQManager identifies a mistake, he seeks to discover its cause, often starting with the employee. He begins by putting the employee at ease, making sure the employee understands that the purpose is not to place blame, but to discover the cause of the mistake and to develop a course of action to correct the problem. The focus is on the issue, with the goal of finding solutions, not assigning blame. Does the employee understand what is expected? Was the mistake caused by an attitude or ability issue ("won't do" versus "can't do")? Are the reasons external to the immediate work situation (supplier problems, family problems, or problems with another team member)? The TQManager works with the employee until

- The root cause is identified.
- A corrective action is developed that will prevent the mistake from recurring.
- They have mutually agreed-upon objectives, standards, and measurements that provide the employee with specific, measurable objectives and actions.
- The employee knows not only how to correct the problem for the future, but how to learn from the experience.

KEY BEHAVIORS THAT SUPPORT OPENNESS AND TRUST

To achieve openness and trust, the TQManager will do the following:

Continue to...

- Be responsible for results
- Communicate
- Evaluate performance
- Give instructions
- Provide good working conditions

Do more...

- Listening to colleagues and subordinates
- Empowering

- Teaching and coaching
- Separating the "sin" from the "sinner"
- Communicating in all directions
- Following through in a supportive, rather than an evaluative, mode
- Looking for both incremental improvements and breakthroughs in processes
- Understanding the potential value of collaboration

Do less . . .

- Directing and controlling or ordering
- Singling out individuals for reward or recognition

Start . . .

- Building a climate of trust as a priority task

Stop . . .

- Blaming others for mistakes

YOUR PERSONAL PLAN FOR BUILDING OPENNESS AND TRUST

At this point it might be helpful for you to review your answers and assessments in Exhibit 3.1. On the basis of our discussion about openness and trust and your earlier reflections, you may wish to consider what steps you want to take in order to make changes for the future. Use the form in Exhibit 3.2.

SUMMARY COMMENTS

There is very little difference between what is expected of managers in a TQM organization and what is expected in

Exhibit 3.2. Notes on Openness and Trust.

Now that I have read the chapter on openness and trust and reviewed my answers to the reflections in Exhibit 3.1, there are some personal actions I want to take to create a work environment in which members of my team can be more open and trustful of me and one another. Therefore, I will do the following:

- Continue to . . . _____

  _____

  _____

- Do more . . . _____

  _____

  _____

- Do less . . . _____

  _____

  _____

- Start . . . _____

  _____

  _____

- Stop . . . _____

  _____

  _____

- Seek feedback on . . . _____

  _____

  _____

  _____

other organizations. The fundamentals do not change. The constant drive for a respectable profit and return on assets is the dominant focus, and there is an increasing demand for good "people managers." There is no revolution in the *what* and the *why* of management. Only the *how* changes—but that change can be dramatic.

The need to filter the massive amounts of information that flow through organizations in the new economy mandates that this processing be done by teams with the charter to monitor, condense, and organize quick, correct actions. In turn, teams need conscientious leaders who place a high value on interpersonal skills, openness, and trust. The old master-servant relationships are gone in TQM organizations, as are the superheroes and lone guns who used to do it all for a corporation only a few years ago. They have been replaced by TQManagers.

These new managers develop environments of openness and trust, and they have the confidence to take an occasional risk. They are comfortable with risk takers and recognize and reward people with good ideas, even when some of them fail. TQManagers are open to a broader spectrum of personalities, skills, and professional backgrounds in their circle of advisers and colleagues. Successful TQManagers have learned to use openness and trust to lower the drawbridge between themselves and their employees so that valuable ideas may cross over and triumph.

4

Two:
Building Collaboration
and Teamwork

There is something exciting and energizing about being a member of a dynamic, successful team. It's more fun to go to work. It's comforting and encouraging to know that you have colleagues who are working together to achieve the same goal. "No one of us is as smart as all of us" is a truism, and it is accepted as an increasingly important guideline for TQManagers.

The objective of TQM is to engage everyone in the organization in a totally integrated effort toward improving performance at all levels. This means bringing managers and individual contributors together in teams, not just the usual working relationships, but teams that recognize their inter-dependence and value collaboration.

TQManagers facilitate this transition by providing their people with greater influence over their work and by encouraging *all* their employees to participate in problem-solving and quality-improvement activities. By doing this, TQManagers provide their people with true empowerment. In return, the TQManager gains the benefit of the creativity, innovation, and commitment of the people closest to the work.

REFLECTIONS ON COLLABORATION AND TEAMWORK

Thanks to the research that has been done during the last half century, we have some very clear guidelines about what makes a good team and what you can do to build teamwork. This chapter brings some of that research into focus to help you become a better team member and team leader.

Again, we suggest that you pause here to reflect on your own experience with teams, using Exhibit 4.1.

THE RELEVANCE OF COLLABORATION AND TEAMWORK

There are great rewards to be realized by working in groups and finding new and better ways of doing things. However, while experience teaches us that working collaboratively offers exciting possibilities, capturing such excitement is hard work. The TQManager may have to learn how to teach her team to work together by helping them identify their objectives and clarify their team's purpose; the manager must also learn the skills of collaboration. This means helping the team members to understand four major factors:

1.   Their mission and the outputs they create to support that mission

2.   The customer for their outputs

3.   That customer's requirements

4.   How to use their interdependence

Exhibit 4.1. Reflections on Collaboration and Teamwork.

1. Think about the best team you were ever on:
    - What did you like most about being a member? _____

    - How were you recruited for the team? _____

    - What did the team leader do that helped to weld
      the members into a group? _____

2. Now think about how you behave as the leader of your work team. In
    responding to the items below, use the following scale:

	Almost Never	Rarely	Sometimes	Frequently	Almost Always
Note: Some of these statements can be regarded as positive, others as negative.					
I try to act like the most responsible member of the team.	—	—	—	—	—
I spend more time praising the efforts of individual members of the team than praising the team as a whole.	—	—	—	—	—
I believe in teamwork, but I am troubled by the amount of time my people spend in meetings.	—	—	—	—	—
I encourage competition among my employees.	—	—	—	—	—
I avoid team meetings whenever I can.	—	—	—	—	—
I believe that teams are almost always more creative and productive than individuals.	—	—	—	—	—
When a complex problem arises, I tend to think first about which group of employees or colleagues could deal with it.	—	—	—	—	—
I make every effort to recognize team effort, rather than singling out individuals.	—	—	—	—	—
Members of my work group feel free to speak up when I disagree with a decision.	—	—	—	—	—
My work group has the equipment, tools, and training necessary to function as a team.	—	—	—	—	—

*After you have finished reading this chapter, return to this chart, review your
responses, and make notes on how you might want to change.*

But it doesn't stop there. The TQManager must also provide the tools and resources the team members need to meet their customers' requirements and must make certain that they are properly motivated to get the job done. To help achieve these goals, TQManagers participate in their team's endeavors and share responsibilities as would any partner. They sit in on team meetings and make themselves available to assist the team in any way necessary.

John Naisbitt and Patricia Aburdene (1985, p. 52) described the importance of managers' development of their teams in *Re-inventing the Corporation:* "We used to think that the manager's job was to know all the answers. But in the 1980's, the new manager ought, rather, to know the questions, to be concerned about them and involve others in finding answers. Today's manager needs to be more of a facilitator—someone skilled in eliciting answers from others—sometimes from people who do not even know that they know." TQManagers know that people are capable of accepting much more responsibility than they are usually given credit for, because they are smarter, more knowledgeable, and more capable than many people may think.

Teamwork cannot survive without interteam and intra-team communication. First, as in any team, members must be able to communicate with one another. Second, as they develop this new way of working, they will need contact with other teams to obtain data on comparable work processes as well as for reinforcement. To be able to facilitate these needs, TQManagers have to participate in their team's activities, be encouraging at team meetings, share timely performance feedback with the team, and stimulate cross-functional team development. Even more important, they have to facilitate agreement on jointly held but noncompetitive goals for the team's members.

Competition sometimes prods people to do their best. It energizes and adds drama to many human endeavors. For example, track records are usually broken in competitive settings. It is quite natural, then, to see competition in the workplace when a department or division tries to become recognized as the best. Sometimes top management encourages this type of rivalry, assuming that everyone will try harder to win. The strategy may work, but it also has a downside. If I am in competition with you, it may make it more difficult for me to view you as a colleague. I may even begin to view you as a rival, an opponent, or merely someone to defeat. When that happens, as we have seen in many organizations, people find subtle ways of working against each other, withholding information that might help others or trying to undermine their reputation with the boss. And, of course, where there are winners, there are also losers.

Organizations committed to Total Quality do not encourage that kind of rivalry. Instead, the emphasis is on teamwork — collaboration between departments, collaboration with customers and suppliers, collaboration between union and management.

HELPING AND BLOCKING FACTORS FOR BUILDING COLLABORATION AND TEAMWORK

A manager who wants to adopt the personal practices that will lead to collaboration and teamwork must first focus on those few vital behaviors that will best help in achieving this goal. At the same time he will have to be aware of the behaviors that will block his progress. These behaviors are outlined in Figure 4.1.

HELPING FACTORS: FIVE THINGS THE TQMANAGER CAN DO

Recognize and Use the Power of Teamwork

The fuel of Total Quality is teamwork. After all the processes and tools of Total Quality have been learned, it is all for

Figure 4.1. Building Collaboration and Teamwork.

AS IS - ➤ SHOULD BE

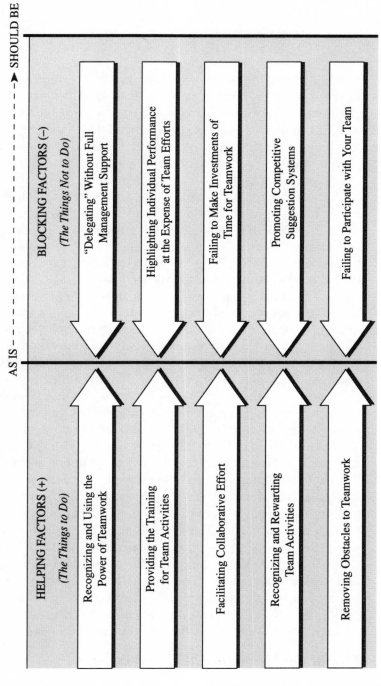

HELPING FACTORS (+)
(The Things to Do)

Recognizing and Using the
Power of Teamwork

Providing the Training
for Team Activities

Facilitating Collaborative Effort

Recognizing and Rewarding
Team Activities

Removing Obstacles to Teamwork

BLOCKING FACTORS (−)
(The Things Not to Do)

"Delegating" Without Full
Management Support

Highlighting Individual Performance
at the Expense of Team Efforts

Failing to Make Investments of
Time for Teamwork

Promoting Competitive
Suggestion Systems

Failing to Participate with Your Team

nothing if people do not work together. "No one of us is as smart as all of us" is the motto of teamwork because Total Quality is a clear example of the whole being greater than the sum of the parts. However, experienced TQManagers know that harnessing the power of groups takes more than a catchy phrase and the mere formation of a team. They know, for example, that individuals can improve work processes and quality, but that the real gains come from a team's collective efforts to solve problems and determine the best work process. They also know that real success depends upon the leadership and support provided for team activities. And they know that for some employees, TQM may be their first experience in formal sessions to discuss work-related issues.

TQManagers are sensitive and supportive of those who are not accustomed to sharing their ideas in public or speaking in groups, and they are aware that too often employees think that being part of a team requires them to sacrifice themselves for the team's goals. It is not uncommon for employees to question their ability to contribute when someone comes along who they think can do the job better. Rather than fully using their assets, these employees believe that they are being team players when they pull back and let someone else take their place. That kind of thinking just won't work in TQM and it is the TQManager's job to convince all of her employees to think and act differently, to see and experience the power of collaboration, where people do not merely value conformity and getting along, but also examine different points of view with one another. TQManagers encourage their people to use, rather than suppress, their thoughts and feelings to help shape their shared boundary conditions. Once their strengths and weaknesses are better known and their roles and responsibilities are clearly stated, the TQManager helps the team create the basis for a flexible team system that *negotiates* roles and responsibilities and focuses on business objectives.

Provide the Training for Team Activities

To be effective at managing their work, employees must have training in the tools and processes necessary to improve their work methods and interteam deliberations. One of the hall-marks of TQM is the consistency with which processes and tools are applied throughout the organization. It is the TQManager's responsibility to be certain that all of her people have been trained to use the organization's common quality tools as well as to know any specialized technical skills that may be required by an individual's job. To be effective at evaluating the team's learning, the TQManager must know the basic concepts of Total Quality and its tools and processes, just like everyone else, but also must learn the skills needed for managing with quality tools and develop a process for inspecting the team's work processes. It is this expertise that allows the TQManager to facilitate employees' quality applications on the job. When the manager actively joins the team in learning and applying the tools of Total Quality, she shows her commitment both to teamwork and to the team's growth. This kind of involvement in the team's learning will help them grasp their interdependence and the value of their teamwork. What invariably follows is an expansion of the team's creativity and the discovery of new and improved work processes.

Facilitate Collaborative Effort

The transition to TQM is not easy, and the transition to teamwork takes time and encouragement. TQManagers help their employees make the transition from being a cluster of individuals to acting as a team by facilitating, coaching, and supporting them in their problem-solving, quality-improvement, and collaborative activities. TQManagers provide their teams with direction and guidance. As their facilitator, they guide the teams in their meeting process and structure. As their teacher and coach, they assist the teams in choosing methods for reviewing their targets, work processes, and plan variances. This means teaching and coaching the teams to monitor their work systems and performance, based on hard evidence. The TQManager educates his team to identify the causes behind the facts by finding out *how, why,* and *what.*

Because the TQManager understands that the people who do the work know it better than those who supervise, he establishes expectations that the team members will become involved in solving their own work problems. He does this by

- Continually working at initiating and building the team's skills

- Recognizing and rewarding their problem-solving and quality-improvement activities

- Identifying strategic and tractical problems for them to pursue

- Joining with them as a collaborator

Decision making in groups can be tough. It is the TQManager's job to help the team find a position acceptable enough so that everyone can live with it—in other words, *consensus.* This does not mean a unanimous vote, since the team decision may not represent everyone's first priority. Similarly, it does not mean a majority vote, because when majority rules, only the majority are happy. Instead, the TQManager seeks to establish a state of affairs where communication has been open, the group climate has been supportive, and all group members feel they have had a fair chance to influence the outcome. In TQM, consensus is a clear course of action to which most members subscribe, one that the dissenters will support because they feel they have had their chance to influence the outcome.

TQManagers learn how to facilitate by developing the skills and characteristics of coaches. They focus on their team members' interpersonal and work process skills, and like a coach, they want to be certain that these skills are honed to their full potential. Very simply, the facilitator's job is to help the team free itself from internal obstacles so that it can efficiently and effectively pursue its desired goals. In the purest sense, when the TQManager is wearing the facilitator's hat, she acts as a "neutral servant" of the team. She focuses on

- Guiding without directing
- Bringing about action without disruption
- Helping the team discover new approaches
- Eliminating the walls between people while preserving structures of value

As a facilitator, the TQManager strives to evaluate her team's progress against five criteria:

1. *Team integrity:* How well are the team's goals understood and actively supported? Do the team's goals contribute to organizational goals? Are meetings consistently well attended? Are team behaviors constructive and productive?

2. *Process discipline:* Does the team use a disciplined, structured approach to problem solving? Does it use the quality tools appropriately? Does it pursue quality improvement in its work processes?

3. *Results:* Does the team implement and evaluate its solutions, using verifiable feedback mechanisms? Can the team communicate its complete problem-solving or quality-improvement activity in a clear way? Can its accomplishments be understood in terms of dollars saved, time saved, customer satisfaction, or quality improvement measured?

4. *Innovation:* Has the team incorporated at least one element of newness or creativity in its work process?

5. *Team development and growth:* Is there a supportive group climate? Does the team demonstrate mastery of the organization's tools, processes, and techniques, including interpersonal behaviors and meeting processes?

The TQManager also facilitates the team's dialogue with other teams, in which it obtains data on comparable work

processes and shares experiences for both learning and reinforcement. A TQManager sees the facilitator's role as

- Requiring learning and personal use of the tools and
  processes of Total Quality
- Facilitating the team's collaboration by using team-
  building techniques and effective meeting skills
- Looking for opportunities for the team to work on common problems

Recognize and Reward Team Activities

One of our greatest sources of satisfaction in life, regardless of
what our responsibilities may involve, is to be told on a regular
basis that our work is appreciated. When times are rough, a
word of encouragement is often the incentive that keeps us
trying. When we are doing well, recognition of our efforts can
inspire us to even higher levels of achievement. Because the
world of work is prominent in the lives of most of us (many of
us spend more waking hours in our work environments than
we do at home with our families), the way we are treated at
work has a powerful effect on the way we feel about ourselves
as individuals, and it clearly affects our work performance.

A TQManager knows the importance of establishing a
work atmosphere of confidence, respect, and mutual trust,
because such an atmosphere fosters the development of personally satisfying work relationships. A positive work environment ensures that people are encouraged and motivated to
practice Total Quality. People want to do well on the job and
need to "belong"; thus they seek close team relationships with
peers and their boss. The TQManager knows that it is his job
to meet these expectations by acknowledging and appreciating employee support for Total Quality, teamwork, and
commitment.

TQManagers know the importance of *recognition*,
whether it takes the form of a simple "thank you" or an
honorary title like Team Captain, and do not underestimate
its power. They know that *reward*, on the other hand, is tangi-

ble, such as money, a plaque, or a gift. And they know that reward without recognition has little lasting value. Sometimes TQManagers use special awards and cash bonuses for teams and individuals, incentive plans to promote the use of quality processes and the achievement of results, and general bonus plans (or other group plans like gainsharing), all of which enable employees to participate in the financial benefits of Total Quality. Whatever awards they use, TQManagers make certain that

- The team knows that such programs exist.
- The team understands the criteria for receiving an award.
- Team members perceive that they have the ability to meet the criteria.
- Recognition-and-reward programs are utilized.
- Team members receive awards that are consistent with their quality objectives and accomplishments.
- Recognition and reward are given in a timely manner.

Remove Obstacles to Teamwork

The TQManager helps the expansion of teamwork and collaboration by removing the four most common obstacles that stand in a team's way:

1. She reduces resistance to change by spelling out the advantages of teamwork, such as quality improvement, enhanced creativity, improved quality of work life, increased efficiency, and more flexibility in the workplace.
2. He makes certain that his team has the training and skills to function as a team. This includes a method of identifying the customer's requirements, a problem-solving process, interpersonal skills that help the team to work collaboratively, and guidelines and skills to ensure efficient processing of the work.

3.   She makes certain that her team has the resources it needs to accomplish its tasks, including functional knowledge and skills, tools, funding, time away from the work area for meetings, and facilities for meetings.

4.   He makes certain that his organization's compensation programs do not work *against* collaboration and teamwork. As an example, do the organization's suggestion programs allow for team awards? Do performance appraisals take into account that an individual's performance is dependent on team behaviors?

BLOCKING FACTORS: FIVE THINGS THE TQMANAGER SHOULD NOT DO

Don't "Delegate" Without Giving Full Management Support

The TQManager's role differs from the traditional concept of a "boss." Traditional American managers sometimes find it hard to give ownership and responsibility to others; in their book, *Managing for Excellence: The Guide to Developing High Performance in Contemporary Organizations*, David Bradford and Allan Cohen (1984, pp. 10–11) identified four "myths" that contribute to this attitude:

1.   The good manager knows at all times what is going on in the department.

2.   The good manager should have more technical expertise than any subordinate.

3.   The good manager should be able to solve any problem that comes up.

4.   The good manager should be the primary person responsible for how the department is working.

TQManagers know that they cannot have all the answers — in fact, they know it is a challenge even to know some of the *questions*! They also recognize that the people who do the work not only possess effective skills, but are closer to the day-to-day realities of the work process. For these reasons, once they have provided the skills and processes of Total Quality to their employees, TQManagers are quick to delegate responsibility. They know that the sooner employee teams start grappling with their work-related problems, the sooner solutions will begin to reap rewards in quality improvements.

But TQManagers also know that delegating responsibility and accountability is not abandonment. Like individuals, teams grow slowly and need guidance and watching to assess both their ability and their willingness to do the job. TQManagers know that they cannot walk away and come back in three months to see how the team is doing. Instead, they have to stay with their team and obtain the resources, skills, and information needed to accomplish the task. They exert their leadership by facilitating and coaching their team. The TQManager delegates, but only with full management support.

Don't Highlight Individual Performance at the Expense of Team Effort

The pay systems of many organizations require a prescribed distribution of appraisal results that usually lead to the stack ranking of co-workers. This can create two problems: (1) the workers feel as if they are being viewed as numbers, rather than as individuals who have been objectively assessed in terms of their skill, achievement, and contribution to the business; and (2) competitiveness among individuals is encouraged. Stack ranking encourages individual performance, but it does not promote the teamwork that is necessary for achieving group results. To counter this problem, the primary focus of performance appraisals in TQM is recognition of both the accomplishment of results and the use of quality tools and processes, including collaborative behaviors.

Individual performance-appraisal systems can easily destroy the accomplishments of teamwork if they encourage people to focus on individual goals rather than the organization's goals. TQManagers know this. They also know that people are not always directly and solely responsible for their performance results, recognizing that most performance variations are caused by the work system and that variations in work systems can be reduced by group objectives. So they try to establish team, or group, objectives that focus the team's attention on the actions that reduce variations in the work process. This requires the TQManager to rethink how she defines and manages failure. TQManagers learn to differentiate between productive and nonproductive failure; as an example, a good plan may have a bad outcome, but if learning takes place and the mistake is not critical, it cannot be considered a productive failure.

Don't Fail to Invest Time in Teamwork

To succeed, teamwork requires an investment of resources, management commitment, and *time*, by both the employee and the manager.

Meetings are an essential element of teamwork — and meetings require time, especially when TQM is first launched and a team is still developing its collaborative skills. For this reason patience is an essential element for launching TQM. When teams are just getting started and are struggling with their group processes, they consume a lot of time. At this point it will seem easier for managers to identify the solutions to problems unilaterally, without team process. Successful TQManagers resist this temptation and demonstrate patience, because they know that time away from the job for meetings and data gathering will be repaid many times over in increased productivity and gains from continuous quality improvement. That is why TQManagers are committed to teamwork and are willing to invest the time to support their team's collaborative sessions.

Don't Promote Competitive Suggestion Systems

TQManagers use every available means to elicit employee ideas for improving quality, and they provide prompt feedback for these ideas. This includes suggestion systems, open comment programs, executive roundtables, and management interviews. But TQManagers know that it is important for the difference between individual and group contributions to be clearly understood. *Individual contributions* make sense when

- The population is geographically dispersed.
- The work is not interdependent.
- Existing financial rewards do not foster cooperation.
- The emphasis is on capturing existing ideas.

Group contributions are appropriate when

- The work is highly interdependent.
- The organization wants a forum to generate ideas and solve problems.
- The fine-tuning of ideas is important.
- Reducing resistance to change is desirable, management would like to focus on specific work problems, and creativity is desired.

Group suggestions are not likely to occur without specific structures such as opportunity, recognition, and support to facilitate them. An organization committed to group contributions must implement appropriate processes to achieve its objective. One way to accomplish this is to set up "idea committees" to receive and evaluate submissions. Another is to provide special incentives or recognition for group contributors.

Don't Fail to Participate with Your Team

From a managerial standpoint, having the employees organized into a team does not diminish the manager's assigned responsibilities, compromise his ability to make tough decisions, or weaken his ability to lead. Participating with employees in a team setting is not being soft, but failing to participate with them will raise doubts about authority, direction, and purpose. Simply put, participating with the team never compromises the TQManager's ability to manage the group, because as the formal leader, he always retains full responsibility for the team's performance and for seeing that the team achieves its objectives. Actually, having this full responsibility affords the TQManager the opportunity to better influence outcomes. By not participating, the manager sends the signal that the team is not important, the manager is not willing to share power, or both.

KEY BEHAVIORS THAT SUPPORT COLLABORATION AND TEAMWORK

To achieve collaboration and teamwork, the TQManager will do the following:

Continue to . . .

- Be responsible for results
- Communicate
- Evaluate performance
- Give instructions
- Provide good working conditions

Do more . . .

- Listening to colleagues and subordinates
- Teaching and coaching
- Encouraging and rewarding team efforts
- Separating the "sin" from the "sinner"
- Communicating in all directions

- Following through in a supportive, rather than an evaluative, mode
- Learning how to participate in meetings and making them productive
- Seeing the potential value of collaboration

Do less...

- Directing and controlling
- Singling out individuals for reward or recognition

Start...

- Assuming that priority attention must be given to process
- Assuming that improvement is more important than maintenance
- Focusing on prevention by inspecting the process, rather than the finished product
- Seeing the potential value of collaboration, for example, in meetings

Stop...

- Basing decisions on experience and status alone
- "Preaching," exhorting, and depending on the power of words alone

YOUR PERSONAL PLAN FOR BUILDING COLLABORATION AND TEAMWORK

At this point it might be helpful for you to review your answers to the questions in Exhibit 4.1. On the basis of our discussion about collaboration and teamwork and your earlier assessment, you may wish to consider steps you want to make in order to adjust your behavior. Use the form in Exhibit 4.2.

Exhibit 4.2. Notes on Collaboration and Teamwork.

Now that I have read the chapter on collaboration and teamwork and reviewed my answers to the reflections in Exhibit 4.1, there are some personal actions I want to take that will help my team and me to forge ourselves into a more productive whole. Therefore, I will do the following:

- Continue to... _____

  _____

  _____

- Do more... _____

  _____

  _____

- Do less... _____

  _____

  _____

- Start... _____

  _____

  _____

- Stop... _____

  _____

  _____

- Seek feedback on... _____

  _____

  _____

  _____

  _____

SUMMARY COMMENTS

Changing the way we do our jobs is sometimes difficult. Changing an organization's culture is almost always difficult to do, but it is necessary. Survival and success in the 1990s depend upon improving employees' effectiveness and increasing productivity and profitability through collaboration and teamwork. How well managers and employees work together to solve problems and how well they use their time will determine an organization's effectiveness. A collaborative approach to information sharing, problem solving, and decision making can clearly produce a higher level of accomplishment and customer satisfaction; the tools to achieve these goals emphasize teamwork and consensus through facilitation and good meeting management.

The TQManager's challenge is to maximize the contributions of employees to ensure that a team's full potential is applied to solving the problem or accomplishing the task. At a minimum it will require a shift from centralized, top-down, autocratic problem solving and decision making to a decentralized, disciplined, and collaborative approach.

5

Three:
Managing by Fact

Managers are expected to know how to make decisions both as individuals and as members of a team. Some of these decisions involve planning—determining goals that are realistic and deciding on ways to reach them—and some involve solving problems—identifying causes and proposing new systems to prevent errors in the future. In a very stable world, the manager may well have encountered a particular problem before and have experience on which to draw. However, in today's fast-moving world, the manager often encounters problems for which there are no pretested models. The challenge is to gather the right kind of data to describe the situation, analyze it, and develop a set of measurable goals and processes.

TQManagers learn to use the tools and processes of Total Quality in their decision making (see the resources in Chapter Nine). They know how to query team members on their use of the tools, and also how to base their actions and decisions on data that has been identified from the root cause of a problem or the root source of a continuous improvement opportunity. TQManagers learn to base their actions, not simply on intuition or what *appears* to be correct, but on quantifiable evidence.

REFLECTIONS ON MANAGING BY FACT

This chapter deals with your decision-making style. It focuses particularly on your use of the tools and techniques developed in TQM. As we look at the role of the manager in the turbulent, fast-changing 1990s, we begin to understand that the manager can only achieve business results through empowering her team and managing the business processes on the basis of proven facts and data. There is no time for rework!

Again we suggest that you reflect for a few minutes on your own approach to a decision-making style, using Exhibit 5.1.

THE RELEVANCE TO TQM OF MANAGING BY FACT

Most managers see the work process in simple, obvious terms. They believe, therefore, in simple, obvious solutions to problems. This usually leads to a frenzied search for simple fixes and a kind of find-and-fix mentality that results in an endless stream of short-term fixes. Each time a fix appears to make a problem go away, but problems keep returning and we have to go off and fix them again. It is the application of this find-and-fix process to multiple-simultaneous, interdependent cause-effect-cause relationships that accounts for a great deal of why managers are so drawn to simple solutions. For example, if an organization has a problem with long product development times, the response is usually to hire more engineers. If the problem is low profits, the reaction is to cut costs — and the response to falling market share is to cut prices. What should be at question is whether the root causes of the problems have been identified and whether the fix is the correct solution.

The object of TQM is to satisfy the customer's require-

Exhibit 5.1. Reflections on Managing by Fact.

---

1. Recall a situation in which you had to resolve a difficult problem and answer these questions:

   - Did you spend much time thinking about the problem's *cause*, or did you immediately focus your attention on *what to do about it?* _____

   - How quantitative was the data available to you regarding the problem and/or the solution you chose? _____

   - Did you know whether your solution was a good one? _____

2. Check your own behavior. How often is each of these statements true of you?

	Almost Never	Rarely	Sometimes	Frequently	Almost Always
Note: Some of these statements can be regarded as positive, others as negative.					
I understand and use the TQM tools for identifying and analyzing problems.	—	—	—	—	—
My team and I try to simplify the way we do our work.	—	—	—	—	—
I use quality-improvement processes to review business performance and results.	—	—	—	—	—
My team has the authority to make changes in its work process to improve performance.	—	—	—	—	—
My team knows how to quantify customers' requirements.	—	—	—	—	—
Most of what we do in my organization has been determined by tradition.	—	—	—	—	—
I seek my team's input on workload and priorities.	—	—	—	—	—
We always seem to be in too big a hurry to get things done right in my organization.	—	—	—	—	—
We have a tendency to accept a simple definition of a problem.	—	—	—	—	—
I inspect my team's work processes, not just their results.	—	—	—	—	—

After you have finished reading this chapter, return to this chart, review your responses, and make notes on how you might want to change.

---

ments and to do so correctly, without error, the first time through. Since most of us have not managed this way before (our experience has been to find and fix), we are accustomed to use "diagnostics" and "cures" based on what has worked in the past. Too often we have not been taught to see our job as finding new cures, much less permanent cures (pursuing errorless work processes), but that is what TQM is all about. Total Quality demands problem assessment based on facts to uncover the real cause of a problem and to identify solutions that will work over the long term. Total Quality also demands implementation plans that have been evaluated and modeled to ensure that they will work. Intuition and prior experience, in and of themselves, are no longer enough — TQManagers do more! John Manoogian, general manager of the Alpha division of Ford Motor Company, put it plainly: "We simply cannot achieve and maintain our goals of leadership in quality, cost, and ontime programs without continuously improving the processes we use to conduct our business" (Rummler, 1991, p. 59).

Most of us would agree that the major objective of managers is to ensure that the organization meets its operational goals. In the 1990s and beyond, organizations will meet their business objectives through empowered work teams that will stabilize and improve their work processes by the use of *verifiable information* and *statistical tools*. As we have previously discussed, the TQManager's job is to provide the training and facilitation to establish and maintain the team's focus on the right objectives, and to help the team maintain a stable work process so that variations from the acceptable limits can be identified.

The first thing TQManagers do is to make certain that their team has had the correct training in the use of data and statistical tools. It is the manager's responsibility to be familiar with the kinds of information a team will use — hard data, soft data, and experiential data — in order to help the team understand how such information is used. Hierarchically, these information sources are

- *Hard data:* Information obtained from statistical processes and substantiated facts, such as engineering experiments like the Taguchi method (see Taguchi in Resource C)

- *Soft data:* Information gleaned from anecdotal sources or observed phenomena

- *Experiential data:* Information based on experience or education

The objective of the management-by-fact style is to achieve the organization's business results through continuous work process improvement, based on the most quantifiable data available. Whatever their data sources, the work team applies statistical tools in the following sequence:

1.   They evaluate the variations in the work processes.
2.   They evaluate alternative solutions to correct the variation.
3.   They select the appropriate solution.
4.   They evaluate the effectiveness of the solution's implementation.

A team does this, not only because it has been empowered to do so, but because this is what management *expects.* Because management can "expect what it inspects," TQManagers become personally familiar with the use of statistical tools and quality processes so that they can inspect their team's work activities and progress toward continuous improvement. This places management by fact at the heart of the role of the TQManager.

HELPING AND BLOCKING FACTORS FOR MANAGING BY FACT

A manager who wants to adopt the personal practices that will lead to management by fact must first focus on the few vital behaviors that will best help to achieve this goal. At the same time, he will have to be aware of behaviors that may block his progress (see Figure 5.1).

HELPING FACTORS: FIVE THINGS THE TQMANAGER CAN DO

Use the Tools and Processes of Quality

Statistical tools and quality processes are the machinery of Total Quality, providing people with new methods of assessing and performing their work, solving problems, and improving product, service, and process quality. The most common tools used are the seven statistical tools shown in Resource B: cause-and-effect (fishbone) diagrams (Figure B.1), check sheets (Figure B.2), control charts (Figure B.3), flow charts (Figure B.4), histograms (Figure B.6), Pareto charts (Figure B.7), run charts (Figure B.9), and scatter diagrams (Figure B.10).

TQManagers know that the tools and processes of quality give employees the knowledge and skills that let them make TQM work. With these tools employees can determine their critical work processes, identify work process improvements, perform root cause analysis, and pursue improvement opportunities such as cycle time reduction. With a solid footing in statistical tools and processes, employees are able to effectively evaluate their work processes, join with others in teams, and find and eliminate the variabilities that block continuous quality improvement. Some of the instruments that are used are a problem-solving process (Figure B.8), a quality-improvement process, the seven statistical tools, benchmarking, and techniques for collaboration. But TQManagers know that you can't *push* statistics into an organization; you have to create a pull for it by understanding other people's problems and figuring out how you can help them to be more effective in doing their jobs well.

TQManagers need to be aware of the danger that a team

Figure 5.1. Management by Fact.

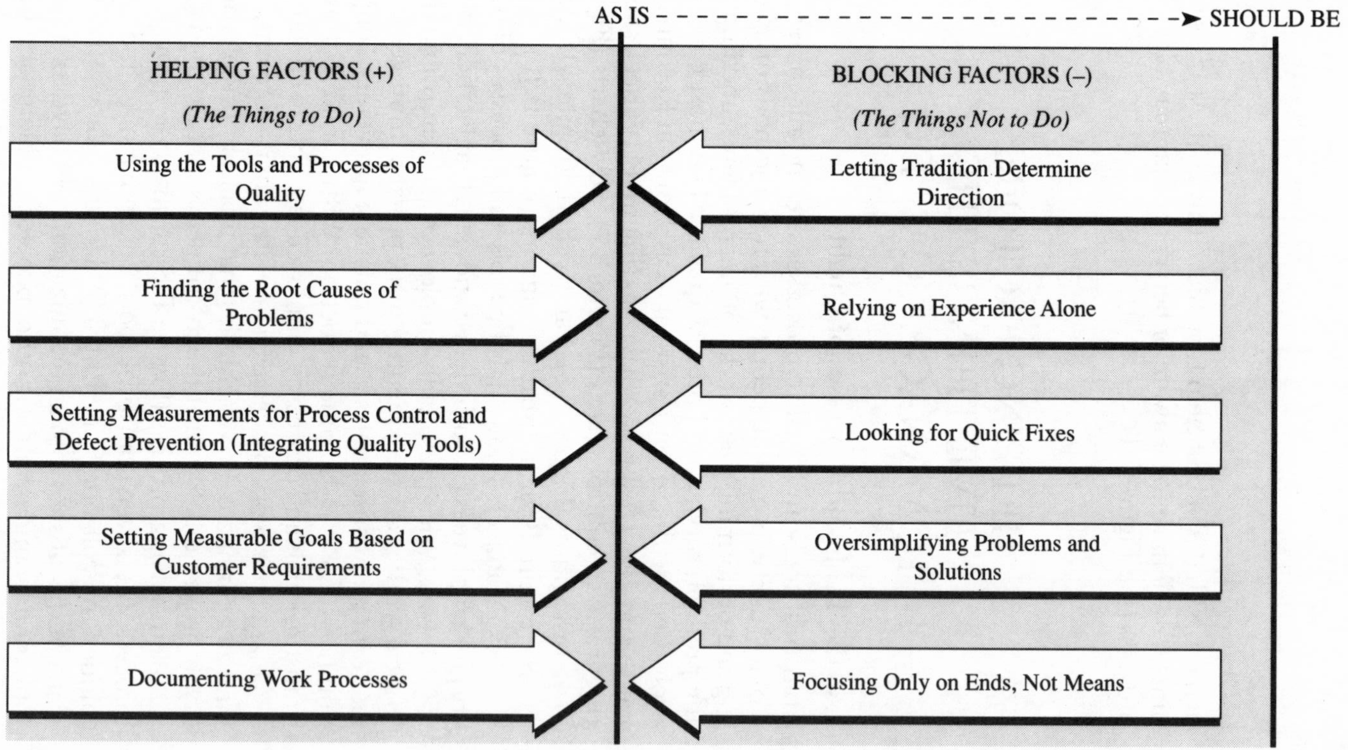

AS IS - → SHOULD BE

BLOCKING FACTORS (−)
(The Things Not to Do)

Letting Tradition Determine Direction

Relying on Experience Alone

Looking for Quick Fixes

Oversimplifying Problems and Solutions

Focusing Only on Ends, Not Means

HELPING FACTORS (+)
(The Things to Do)

Using the Tools and Processes of Quality

Finding the Root Causes of Problems

Setting Measurements for Process Control and Defect Prevention (Integrating Quality Tools)

Setting Measurable Goals Based on Customer Requirements

Documenting Work Processes

that is well versed in the use of statistical tools may think of its early successes as a sign that it has achieved its goal, while under the surface the old behaviors linger, waiting for this latest fad to pass. Still other teams have to guard against becoming too enamored with early gains in style change, like collaborative meeting processes and the use of "soft" tools, such as brainstorming. They, too, may see fast results as success, while their management by fact continues to be overshadowed by the same old decisions for the same old reasons.

Find the Root Causes for Problems

Searching for the root causes of issues means not being satisfied with easy or simplistic answers until the *why* of a problem is answered. This demonstrates the TQManager's style. The repetitive question "Why?" is a powerful tool TQManagers use to uncover the *real* causes of problems with their team's work processes. This commitment to finding the root causes of cause-and-effect issues in work processes not only uncovers opportunities for improvement, but strongly demonstrates what Total Quality is all about.

Most of us have had experience with problems that have been "fixed" only to return. One common example is the car that stops for no apparent reason. After a hefty repair bill it runs again for a day or two (or an hour or two) and inexplicably stops again. Obviously the real cause of the problem eluded the mechanic, but it was the customer who was inconvenienced. This is what TQM tries to avoid. TQManagers use whatever tools and data are available to help their team to identify the root causes, by tracing back through a matrix of all the possible causes until the original ones are found.

A famous saying is relevant here: "For want of a nail, the shoe was lost. For want of a shoe, the horse was lost. For want of a horse, the rider was lost. For want of a rider, the battle was lost. For want of the battle, the war was lost."

Set Measurements for Process Control and Defect Prevention

Organizations get the most benefit when they integrate TQM processes and tools into their normal business processes.

When this happens, TQManagers reinforce the idea that Total Quality can be used to manage planning sessions, operations reviews, long-range planning processes — *all* of the organization's business — today!

James Harrington warns in his book, *Business Process Improvement* (1991, p. 16), "Expending much more effort to improve business processes during the 1990s will be a major factor in being competitive in the twenty-first century." He goes on to suggest that failure to improve business processes may result in undesirable effects: "Processes left unregulated will change, but that change will be for the convenience of the people in the process rather than for the best interest of the organization or the customer."

The goal of TQM is *error prevention*, or *doing things right the first time*. When perfection is not immediately achieved, however, TQManagers guide their teams to this goal by the continuous improvement of their work processes. By measuring the checkpoints in a work process, the team gains four benefits:

1.   Objective evaluation of their work activities

2.   Early identification of problems

3.   The key actions required to meet the output in "real time"

4.   Prevention of errors

Measurement provides the TQManager and her team with process control and the opportunity to prevent defects. By measuring key indicators, teams are able to identify the likely outcomes and to initiate action when their work process will not enable them to meet the customer's requirements. The TQManager places emphasis on in-process control rather than on inspection at the end of the process. Also, searching for the root causes of issues — not being satisfied with easy or simplistic answers until the *why* of a problem is answered — will help to uncover the real causes of problems in the team's work processes. Whichever process is used — quality improvement or problem solving—TQManagers should remember that most are based on Deming's (1986) PDCA (Plan-Do-Check-Act) model (Figure 5.2), and the whole purpose is to provide a road map that employees can follow to produce quality products and deliver quality services, by showing them where to begin and what questions to ask.

Figure 5.2. Deming's PDCA Circle.

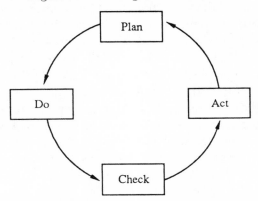

Source: Reprinted from *Out of the Crisis* by W. Edwards Deming by permission of MIT and W. Edwards Deming. Published by MIT, Center for Advanced Engineering Study, Cambridge, MA 02139. Copyright 1986 by W. Edwards Deming.

Set Measurable Goals Based on Customer Requirements

As the organization's basic operating principle, TQM goes to the very heart of the organizational culture. The ultimate goal is to anticipate and respond to the customer's needs in the design and manufacture of the organization's products and services. This means acquiring the best possible understanding of what the customer desires. How will our products or services be used? How are we perceived relative to our competitors? Understanding the customer's requirements is the job of every employee.

It is easy to see how quality improvement can facilitate the achievement of business goals. TQManagers try to make it equally clear that the key is understanding what has to be improved, the customer for the work, and the customer's requirements. The task is to put emphasis on the use of the process to achieve *improved* results rather than results alone.

We have learned from Phil Crosby (1979) and many other TQM experts that the cost of poor quality, or the lack of conformance to quality, is at least 20 percent of sales. (Our studies suggest it is higher in most organizations.) Perhaps the most insidious result of poor quality is lost sales opportunities, which can be difficult to measure. Most companies only measure the number and kind of customer complaints they receive. These organizations don't know how many customers or potential customers didn't like their products or services and went someplace else to do business. TQManagers use their awareness of the cost of poor quality to encourage their teams to better understand their customers' requirements, measure the cost of failing to conform, and track lost opportunities. (Some organizations estimate that it costs five times as much to find a new customer as to maintain an existing one!)

Document Work Processes

Many organizations launch TQM because their focus on the customer has been lost. Over time, the organization has become more inwardly focused, and people do not really understand the impact of their activities on the customer. As a result, the process has become ineffective, out of date, overly complicated, burdened with bureaucracy, labor-intensive, time-consuming, and irritating to management and employees alike. While other managers might accept these processes as a necessary evil, the TQManager knows that this kind of work process is a millstone around his team's neck, hampering its ability to compete.

In order to bring focus and purpose to the process, the TQManager begins by having the team members document their work process. This is most effectively done by using flow charts. A flow chart is a sort of pictorial representation of the steps of a work process (see Figure B.4). Flow charts are helpful for identifying deviations between the actual and ideal paths of any product or service. They provide excellent documentation for evaluating how the various steps of a process relate to one another and for uncovering loopholes that are potential sources of trouble. Flow charts can be used to document anything from the route of an invoice or the flow of materials to the steps of a sales cycle or the servicing of a product.

After documenting a work process, the team is able to focus on improvement opportunities by looking at the following:

- The customer's requirements (Why are we doing this work and how is the customer using what we produce?)

- Ways to predict and control change in the work process (Can we meet the customer's requirements?)

- The interrelationships between the process and the team members (How effective are we?)

- The work process itself

- Ways to prevent errors from occurring in the work system

- How inputs become outputs

- The number of errors that occur and what methods might correct them

BLOCKING FACTORS: FIVE THINGS THE TQMANAGER SHOULD NOT DO

Don't Let Tradition Determine Direction

"But that's the way we've always done it around here." These are common words we have all heard, but they are words that don't fit into TQM. Corning's James Houghton (1987, p. 23) says that to support Total Quality a manager must have "flexibility, a willingness to learn, and the ability to listen." To survive in today's world of fast-moving technologies, take-overs, "arrangements" of convenience, emerging nationalism, and global competition, organizations must constantly adjust to the marketplace, public policy, and society. When something goes wrong with a product before or after its introduction, a competitor does the unexpected, or a new environmental regulation is enacted, TQManagers and their teams are expected to act to solve the problem and bring the system back into balance. What is different here is that traditionally management has acted to restore the organization to the state it was in prior to the problem, adapting to external and internal disruptions quickly to maintain stability and confidence in the organization. In TQM, the solution to problems is collaborative, fact-based, and intended to bring about process improvement.

Perhaps the most significant thing a TQManager does to counter "not invented here" thinking is to push ahead and help the team to learn from its mistakes. When failure occurs, rather than letting the resisters win out and going back to the old way, the TQManager uses the failure as a learning opportunity. She challenges the team to design a better way to fix the problem (including an assessment of the old way). This management attitude not only builds ownership for the process with the team; it helps the team to see the evolutionary advantages of trying new things.

Don't Rely on Experience Alone

TQM is a new style of organizational life, building on several decades of management study, experimentation, and practice. Many features of TQM have been around for a long time. The difference in the 1990s, however, is the *linkage* of these various principles and practices into a coherent new set of standards for operating a modern organization.

TQM is not business as usual. Certainly a TQManager's experiences and knowledge should not be abandoned, but achieving TQM's vision for the future requires doing many things a new way. It requires testing our experience against today's realities—determining our actions, not by what has worked in the past, but by what the *facts* indicate is the proper action today. The investment in time, effort, energy, and dollars may be difficult to make, but the return in process improvements, employee satisfaction, and product and service quality will more than pay back this wise investment.

TQManagers are open with their teams. They may tell them, "Based on *my* experience, this is how *I* would attack this problem." But then they ask the team, "Based on *your* experience, what would *you* do?" And the TQManager challenges his team with "Based on the facts—the evidence you have—what should *we* do?"

Don't Look for Quick Fixes

TQManagers commit time and attention to their team. Although collaboration in solving problems and root cause analysis takes time, the TQManager who makes this investment can expect lasting solutions to problems. TQManagers believe that performance improvement can only be achieved by removing the barriers in the system, identifying the hidden opportunities for breakthroughs that improve work processes and performance. In TQManagement *inspiration* has its place, but it is the *perspiration* of fact-based assessment that produces the results. Deming often remarks during his seminars. "You can beat horses; they run faster for a while. Goals are like hay somebody ties in front of the horse's snout. The horse is smart enough to discover no matter whether he canters or gallops, trots or walks or stands still, he can't catch up with the hay. Might as well stand still" (Walton, 1986, p. 77).

Employees are just as smart as horses. They know when we are serious and when we just want the same old outputs. They know they are good at fixing the problems in their job; they have been doing it for years. And that is what the TQManager wants—to stop fixing the same problem quickly, over and over again. She wants instead to help her team take the longer view to find the real cause of a problem and produce a real solution, one that will last.

Don't Oversimplify Problems and Solutions

Solving problems and pursuing quality improvement are not simple tasks. Teams must first differentiate between *common* causes and *special* causes of problems. Common causes constitute 85 percent of the problems encountered in work and are the fault of the system; they affect the members of a team equally, and they will remain until they are identified and removed by management. Special causes are specific to a particular employee, machine, or work practice; they can be detected by statistical analysis and are usually identified and corrected easily.

TQManagers often think of common causes as being related to *effectiveness* — the ability of the organization to have the right process in place. On the other hand, special causes are related to *efficiency* — how well things are being done. To succeed, an organization must be both effective *and* efficient. This means identifying the right problems and fixing them the right way. TQManagers know that attempts to improve individual performance are useless when the problem lies in the system, where only management can eliminate or reduce the problem's impact. The use of statistical tools by all employees allows for a common method to identify and understand critical problems and manage their solution by fact.

Don't Focus Only on Ends and Ignore Means

Experienced TQManagers have learned that the primary objective of measurement is process control and defect prevention through measuring the key indicators. By identifying the likely outcomes and initiating action when the teamwork process does not meet the requirements, a TQManager is able to ensure that the customer's requirements will be met. The emphasis is on in-process control rather than on inspection at the end of the process. Deming says, "Continual reduction in mistakes, continual improvement of quality, mean lower and lower costs. Less rework in manufacturing. Less waste of materials, machine time, tools, human effort" (Walton, 1986, p. 26).

KEY BEHAVIORS THAT SUPPORT MANAGING BY FACT

To achieve management by fact, the TQManager will do the following:

Continue to...

■   Be responsible for results

Do more...

■   Listening to colleagues and subordinates

■   Empowering

■   Separating the "sin" from the "sinner"

■   Systems thinking

■   Systematic measurement

■   Looking for both incremental improvements and break-throughs in the process

Do less...

■   Isolated problem solving (on the basis of experience versus facts)

Start...

■   Understanding the organization as a system of interdependent relationships

■   Assuming that priority attention must be given to the process

■   Assuming that improvement is more important than maintenance

■   Focusing on prevention by inspecting the process, rather than the finished product

■   Learning from problems

Stop . . .

- Basing decisions on experience and status alone
- "Preaching," exhorting, and depending on the power of words alone

YOUR PERSONAL PLAN FOR MANAGING BY FACT

At this point it might be helpful for you to review your answers to the questions in Exhibit 5.1. On the basis of our discussion about managing by fact and your earlier assessment you may wish to consider steps you want to make in order to adjust your behavior. Use the form in Exhibit 5.2.

SUMMARY COMMENTS

Henry Milewski, project director at the American Suppliers' Institute, says that Total Quality makes "obsolete much of what we have believed [about management] for the last seventy years" (MacFarland, 1990, p. 31). He says that it is turning all we have believed about management and business upside down: "It's a whole new way of thinking; we're looking at an entirely new belief system."

TQManagers understand all the intellectual arguments for giving their employees the capacity to make quality happen, but at the same time they know that this alone will not create a workplace where quality happens consistently. They must establish and maintain their own personal involvement in the evaluation and inspection of the work process, variations in the process, and solutions based on hard, physical evidence. John S. Lloyd, president of Witt Associates, put it well: "Quality is not an accidental outcome. It is always the end

Exhibit 5.2. Notes on Managing by Fact.

Now that I have read the chapter on managing by fact and reviewed my answers to the reflections in Exhibit 5.1, there are some personal actions I want to take that will help my team to identify the root causes of problems and use all the data available to us in selecting the correct solutions. Therefore, I will do the following:

■   Continue to . . . _____

_____

_____

■   Do more . . . _____

_____

_____

■   Do less . . . _____

_____

_____

■   Start . . . _____

_____

_____

■   Stop . . . _____

_____

_____

■   Seek feedback on . . . _____

_____

_____

_____

_____

result of visionary leadership. People create quality through intelligent effort, desire, and skill. The organization that takes aim at quality as a target and makes the deep commitment to strive for quality in its products and services must have outstanding leadership if it is to succeed" (Naval, 1989, p. 112).

6

Four:
Supporting Results Through
Recognition and Rewards

Recognizing and rewarding people is a vital feature of TQM. More than any other management act, recognizing and rewarding employees profoundly affects their motivation and job satisfaction. As a manager, you know that your subordinates and colleagues notice which people and which actions you approve and reward. One important source of your power is your ability to give recognition and rewards to those who contribute most to the achievement of your goals. When your requests or demands are consistent with the rewards you give, you send clear signals of what is expected; when they are inconsistent, people will trust your rewards, not your requests. You can expect what you inspect — and reward!

Unfortunately, managers too often miss their opportunities to express appreciation on a day-to-day basis. Sometimes this is a result of uncertainty about how or when an employee's contributions should be recognized. Sometimes a manager loses sight of the purpose of recognition and provides an employee with a monetary reward while forgetting to say "thank you" or celebrate the event with other employees. TQManagers strive to avoid these mistakes because they know that successful implementation of TQM requires them to communicate and reinforce the kinds of contributions and behaviors that are essential to Total Quality.

As a TQManager, you are interested in developing your team and fostering teamwork among your employees and peers. This means that every time you recognize and reward team effort you are reinforcing the concept in the minds of your colleagues.

REFLECTIONS ON RECOGNITION AND REWARDS

Since most traditional organizations tend to recognize individual, rather than team, achievement, some habits may have to be overcome. To make the discussion in this chapter more meaningful, again we suggest that you take a few minutes to reflect on your personal experience with rewards and recognition, using Exhibit 6.1.

THE RELEVANCE OF RECOGNITION AND REWARDS

TQManagers use every form of recognition and reward at their disposal to encourage teamwork and the positive behaviors of Total Quality. They understand the power of systematic rewards that foster the desired behaviors of TQM, while building policies and practices that ensure their continued use. These managers know how to recognize the activities of individuals while still supporting their team, and they know how to recognize the team without sacrificing the individuals who are part of it. TQManagers also know that changing an organization's culture requires a long-term commitment and

Exhibit 6.1. Reflections on Recognition and Rewards.

1. Think of the last time you received significant recognition or a reward for something you did very well. Who actually gave you the recognition or reward? How did you feel about the whole process (i.e., what did you like and what could have been improved)?

    ■   This made me feel good: _____

    ■   This would have made me feel even better: _____

2. Check your own behavior. How often is each of these statements true of you?

	Almost Never	Rarely	Sometimes	Frequently	Almost Always
Note: Some of these statements can be regarded as positive, others as negative.					
■ I have a clear understanding of my organization's policies on when and how to give recognition and rewards to employees.	—	—	—	—	—
■ I communicate the recognition-and-reward programs that are available in our organization.	—	—	—	—	—
■ I inspect my organization's use of recognition-and-reward programs.	—	—	—	—	—
■ Providing the appropriate award to my team members is important to me.	—	—	—	—	—
■ My team members know how their performance on the job is evaluated.	—	—	—	—	—
■ I have tried to get my employees to recognize that their extra efforts are just part of the job.	—	—	—	—	—
■ I have learned that in the final analysis the only dependable motivator for most people is money.	—	—	—	—	—
■ I reward long-term improvements rather than quick fixes.	—	—	—	—	—
■ I reward process, not merely results.	—	—	—	—	—
■ I deliver my recognition and rewards in a timely manner.	—	—	—	—	—

After you have finished reading this chapter, return to this chart, review your responses, and make notes on how you might want to change.

that recognition and rewards are significant tools in encouraging the new behaviors. These TQManagers use recognition and rewards in a variety of ways.

First, from congratulatory notes and personal achievement presentations to plaques, team T-shirts, quality bulletin boards, and team events, TQManagers *recognize* support for TQM. Perhaps the most powerful thing TQManagers do is remembering to say "thank you." Whatever the recognition these managers provide, it is delivered in a genuine manner — and often. Recognition demonstrates the TQManager's ongoing appreciation and concern for his people and as such it is central to his reward-giving behavior.

TQManagers also *reward* deserving teams or individuals for their support of Total Quality. Cash awards and significant prizes help them to acknowledge outstanding accomplishments and behaviors that send the message: "Quality is important." However, determining the *who, what,* and *how* of such rewards requires careful thought and planning. Because successful TQManagers recognize the power of systematic reward plans to encourage the desired behaviors, they build in to their operating policies, guidelines, and budgets the ongoing use of rewards.

Quality's success depends on the day-to-day activities of all employees and on recognizing and rewarding the behaviors that support the organization's goals. It is also important to remember to recognize managers for implementing Total Quality. Managers at all levels of the organization are involved in using the principles and tools of Total Quality, teaching and evaluating their teams, and inspecting results and outcomes in their area of responsibility. It is important to fully recognize and reward their achievements.

The umbrella objective of a recognition-and-reward strategy is to ensure that quality tools and processes are used, work systems are changed or developed to support quality improvement, and appropriate team behaviors are adopted. Recognition and rewards are key tools that TQManagers must know how to use in order to support TQM.

HELPING AND BLOCKING FACTORS FOR SUPPORTING RESULTS THROUGH RECOGNITION AND REWARDS

A manager who wants to adopt the personal practices that will lead to recognition and rewards must first focus on the few vital behaviors that will best help to achieve this goal. At the same time she will have to be aware of the behaviors that will block her progress (see Figure 6.1).

HELPING FACTORS: FIVE THINGS THE TQMANAGER CAN DO

Understand the Differences Between Recognition and Reward

Recognition is the act of acknowledging, approving, or appreciating an activity or a service. It's helpful to think of recognition in terms of its derivation: *re* means "again" and *cognize* means "to think"; therefore, *recognition* means "to think again." An effective recognition strategy causes people to think again about the value and unique contribution they are bringing to the pursuit of Total Quality.

For TQManagers, recognition is an ongoing activity that doesn't focus only on one particular achievement; nor is it given only at award ceremonies. Because recognition is directed at an individual's self-esteem and social needs, it is an intangible acknowledgment of a person's or team's accomplishments, including

Figure 6.1. Supporting Results Through Recognition and Rewards.

AS IS -➤ SHOULD BE

BLOCKING FACTORS (−)
(The Things Not to Do)

Assuming People Work Only for Money

Treating Extra Effort as Part of the Job

Encouraging Quick Fixes at the Expense of Long-Term Improvements

Recognizing and Rewarding Results Alone

Delaying Reward and Recognition

HELPING FACTORS (+)
(The Things to Do)

Understanding the Differences Between Recognition and Reward

Clarifying and Communicating the Rationale for Recognition-and-Reward Systems

Monitoring and Assessing the Use and Impact of Existing Recognition-and-Reward Programs

Seeking and Identifying Opportunities for Recognition and Reward

Knowing and Understanding Overall Organizational Compensation Policies and Procedures

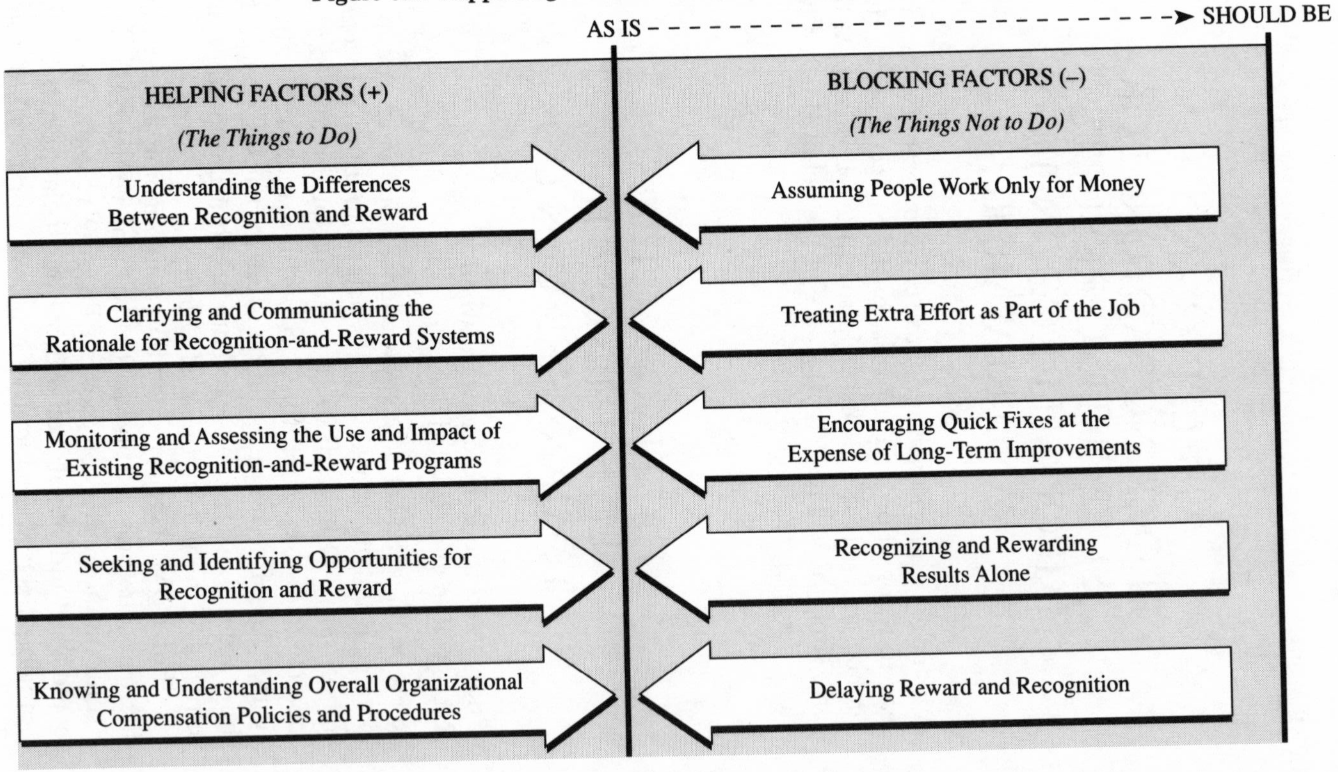

- The feeling of involvement an employee gets when he is asked for his input

- The public expression of appreciation for each person's unique contributions to the team

- Personal "thank you's," letters, mementos, and special lunches or dinners

Reward is the direct delivery of money or something of financial value. In contrast with recognition, rewards punctuate appropriate achievements and serve as manifestations of ongoing recognition. While recognition is an intangible expression of worth, rewards are concrete expressions of appreciation that are meaningful to the receiver. Typical rewards are pay, promotional increases, bonuses, benefits, company cars, profit sharing, and trips. Recognition is always powerful, but reward without recognition is weak. Unfortunately, too often we express appreciation with a plaque or cash award without demonstrating a sincere appreciation of an employee's contributions. When rewards displace recognition, it is a waste of the opportunity and resource.

TQManagers tailor recognition and reward to the unique needs of the people involved. Having a variety of recognition-and-reward options allows managers to appropriately acknowledge their people at different times in different ways. The cliché "Different strokes for different folks" works here. As an example, inviting an employee out to dinner with the boss and her spouse may seem like a nice thing to do, but for some production workers, it may have the opposite effect.

Clarify and Communicate the Rationale for Recognition-and-Reward Systems

TQManagers strive for a clear, unambiguous, and well-communicated "line of sight" between achievements and rewards, because people should understand why they and others receive rewards. This is why TQManagers communicate the recognition-and-reward criteria to everyone, so that people know what is expected of them. It is important for TQManagers to remember that the members of their team know who is doing what, and how well; recognition of individual members of a team has to be consistent with the team's own experience and evaluations.

It is vitally important for the manager to lead employees in making the connection between rewards and activities that support TQM and the organization's goals. After all, a recognition-and-reward policy only makes it possible for managers to acknowledge outstanding performance. The real benefit to the organization, and the real impact on productivity, will materialize when employees perceive that the appraisal of their performance level is accurate and the reward is equitable, and that the reward is, in fact, consistent with what the company is saying. When employees see managers rewarding performance that is deserved, they quickly make the connection that management is serious.

Monitor and Assess the Use and Impact of Existing Recognition-and-Reward Programs

Having recognition-and-reward programs and budgets is not enough; they have to be used! TQManagers make sure that they get feedback and assessment on their use of recognition and reward. This feedback may come from their boss, Human Resources, or even Finance, but at a minimum it tells the TQManager how much recognition-and-reward money has been spent and how much more is available. One-on-one assessments with members of the team and surveys will provide valuable feedback on the effectiveness of your recognition-and-reward actions.

Changing an organization's culture is a long-term commitment. For that reason TQManagers want to use every form of recognition and reward at their disposal to encourage the new behaviors, but at the same time they are careful to use their recognition-and-reward plans realistically. They guard against overuse to keep rewards from becoming so commonplace that they add to the skepticism that often exists in organizations.

Seek and Identify Opportunities for Recognition and Reward

TQManagers place emphasis on success rather than failure. Too often managers miss the positives by busily searching for the negatives. On the other hand, TQManagers search for every opportunity to reinforce positive actions in a warm and personal way, especially during quality start-up when stumbling is certain to occur. TQManagers know that the smallest of successes should be applauded—that any improvement, however small, is movement in the right direction.

Ken Blanchard and Spencer Johnson made the point admirably in their famous allegory, *One Minute Manager* (1982, p. 81). In that book they wrote "Training somebody to become a winner is to catch them doing something right—in the beginning approximately right and gradually moving them towards the desired behavior. With a winner you don't have to catch them doing things right very often, because good performers catch themselves doing things right and are able to be self-reinforcing." In their description of "one minute praisings," they described the success strategy this way:

- Praise the behavior (with true feelings).
- Do it soon.
- Be specific.
- Tell people what they did right.
- Tell them how you feel about it.
- Encourage them (with true feelings).
- Shake hands, and proceed with success.

Know and Understand Overall Organizational Compensation Policies and Procedures

Recognition-and-reward criteria must not only support the goal of Total Quality, but also apply to other corporate policies and objectives. TQManagers are expected to administer their organization's salary programs, policies, and procedures consistently, equitably, and without discrimination. To do this they must be thoroughly familiar with all of them, including those governing salary offers for employment, transfer, reloca- tion, and promotion. Managers must also be familiar with corporate policies on compensation and the organization's guidelines for salary administration, and they must be able to explain benefits and compensation programs to their employ- ees. Employees should know what compensation plans, bonuses, or special incentives are supportive of TQM and know when they conflict with new goals. TQManagers should be prepared to explain any such conflicts, and when they exist, to propose resolutions.

BLOCKING FACTORS: FIVE THINGS THE TQMANAGER SHOULD NOT DO

Don't Assume People Work Only for Money

When people's needs are not fulfilled at work, they may view their jobs as a series of sacrifices and do only what they have to out of obligation. The "I only work here" syndrome may result. When the workplace is responsive to people's needs, they no longer feel as though they are sacrificing. TQManagers strive to create an environment that fosters a setting in which people put passion, energy, excitement, and motivation into their work. They do this by giving their team members the freedom to express how they feel about what is happening at work and to take responsibility for who they are and what they stand for.

Establishing a work climate that goes beyond "labor for hire" will promote employee loyalty and belonging. As part of the Total Quality team, employees have expectations about how they should be treated. It is part of the TQManager's job to meet these expectations by acknowledging and appreciat- ing employee support for Total Quality, teamwork, and commitment; by appropriate recognition and reward; and by fostering a work environment that values interpersonal relations.

Don't Treat Extra Effort as Part of the Job

When he was anchoring the *CBS Evening News,* Walter Cronkite would close the broadcast with "And that's the way it is." It was a simple statement that said that CBS knew what was going on in the world and told the truth about it. Employees expect the same of their bosses — that their manager knows what is going on and is able to tell what is normal, expected behavior, what fails to meet the mark, and what took extra effort.

As we noted earlier, recognizing and rewarding employees profoundly affects their motivation and job satisfaction. This is especially true when they have made a contribution beyond what is expected. Certainly the principle of "a fair day's work for a fair day's pay" is what drives the designers of jobs and compensation programs. It is in keeping with this equitable principle that a TQManager watches for those occasions when an employee provides *more* than "a fair day's work." TQManagers know that efforts beyond the scope of a job are unique achievements that stand out and deserve special recognition.

Don't Encourage Quick Fixes at the Expense of Long-Term Improvements

Recognizing people for their accomplishments has long been an American management principle. But the way some organizations practice this principle is not always as effective as it might be. Deming (1986) has been the most critical in the quality context. The third of his "Seven Deadly Diseases" — "Evaluation of performance, merit rating, or annual review" — says: "It nourishes short-term performance, annihilates long-term planning, builds fear, demolishes teamwork, nourishes rivalry and politics. It leaves people bitter, crushed, bruised, battered, desolate, despondent, dejected, feeling inferior, some even depressed, unfit for work for weeks after receipt of rating, unable to comprehend why they are inferior. It is unfair, as it ascribes to the people in the group differences that may be caused totally by the system that they work in" (p. 98).

The concern here is that short-term thinking at the expense of long-term performance and improvements introduces variability into the work system. In a competitive environment that is becoming increasingly reliant upon teamwork and collaboration, linking performance evaluation and pay delivery to quick fixes or "fighting fires" for short-term gains may in fact be at odds with the goals of continuous improvement.

Rather than fostering interdependence, performance reviews too often encourage people to look out for themselves. In Europe and Japan there are virtually no pay-for-performance systems, so organizations must find other ways to motivate employees. This explains the heavy reliance of the Japanese on participation, involvement, and communication.

Don't Recognize and Reward Results Alone

The very heart of TQM is controlling the quality of the *process*, not the output. Fixing mistakes will not win or retain customers; only when the system, or the process, is in control will the real problems be fixed. When you focus only on results or outcomes, the "line of sight" of the team members will follow and they will begin to focus on results rather than on improving the process that produces the results. So TQManagers go out of their way to provide recognition and rewards not only for results, but for the quality and integrity of the work process that produced the results. The teams of TQManagers who use statistical tools, manage their work processes by fact, and utilize all the talents of the team are usually recognized and rewarded for their efforts.

TQManagers search for every opportunity to reinforce positive actions in a warm and personal way. This includes adhering to the work process and meeting their objectives as both suppliers and customers, especially during quality start-up when stumbling is certain to occur. TQManagers know the value of applauding even the smallest of successes, not just the results. Any improvement, however small, is movement in the right direction.

Don't Delay Recognition and Rewards

TQManagers know the importance and value of a clear, unambiguous, and well-communicated line of sight between an employee's achievement and the reward he receives. For this reason they want others to be aware of the accomplishments of the team and team members. They know that if recognition and rewards are not given publicly and close in time to the actual achievement, they will lose much of their impact. TQManagers deliver their recognition in a personal and honest manner that is appropriate to the individual. Although in a culturally diverse workplace, consideration of an individual's preference should be a factor, TQManagers know that teams are created by celebrations. They strive to match the reward or recognition to the accomplishment and to avoid recognition that is too slick or overproduced, because it distracts from the occasion and the recipient.

KEY BEHAVIORS THAT SUPPORT RESULTS THROUGH RECOGNITION AND REWARDS

To be able to use recognition and rewards most effectively, the TQManager will do the following:

Continue to...

- Evaluate performance
- Provide good working conditions
- Empower employees
- Encourage and reward team efforts

Do more...

- Communicating, in all directions
- Teaching and coaching
- Following through in a supportive, rather than an evaluative, mode

Do less...

- Singling out of individuals for recognition and rewards

Start...

- Looking for more opportunities to reinforce the principles of TQM with recognition and rewards

Stop...

- Blaming others for mistakes
- "Preaching," exhorting, and depending on the power of words alone

YOUR PERSONAL PLAN FOR SUPPORTING RESULTS THROUGH RECOGNITION AND REWARDS

At this point it might be helpful for you to review your answers to the questions in Exhibit 6.1. On the basis of our discussion about recognition and rewards and your earlier assessment, you may wish to consider steps you want to make in order to adjust your behavior. Use the form in Exhibit 6.2.

SUMMARY COMMENTS

As a TQManager, you are interested in developing your team and fostering teamwork among your employees and peers.

Exhibit 6.2. Notes on Recognition and Rewards.

Now that I have read the chapter on recognition and rewards and have reviewed my answers to the reflections in Exhibit 6.1, there are some personal actions I want to take to ensure that I am making the best use of recognition-and-reward programs and opportunities. Therefore, I will do the following:

■ Continue to... _____

_____

_____

■ Do more... _____

_____

_____

■ Do less... _____

_____

_____

■ Start... _____

_____

_____

■ Stop... _____

_____

_____

■ Seek feedback on... _____

_____

_____

_____

_____

Every time you recognize and reward team effort you are reinforcing the concepts of teamwork and Total Quality in the minds of your colleagues.

Quality's success depends on the day-to-day activities of all employees. Recognizing and rewarding their behaviors in supporting the organization's goals play critical roles in the success of TQM.

The umbrella objective of a recognition-and-reward strategy is to ensure that quality tools and processes are used, work systems are changed or developed to support quality improvement, and team behaviors are adopted in support of Total Quality. Recognition and rewards are tools that effective TQManagers know how to use to advance the organization's Total Quality goals and establish the new culture.

7

Five:
Creating a Learning and
Continuously Improving
Organization

Many quality experts argue that the single most important contribution the Japanese have made to the vocabulary of the Quality Revolution is *Kaizen*. As noted earlier, Imai (1986) calls it "the key to Japan's competitive success." It means pursuing gradual unending improvement, doing little things better, and setting and achieving ever higher standards. In this process, everyone in the organization participates through identifying opportunities for improvement, testing out new approaches, recording the results, and recommending changes.

The best support for continuous improvement is an organization of people who give a high priority to learning. Many of today's insights and competencies will be out of date tomorrow. The quest for new ways to think about products, problems, and processes — to develop new paradigms — is going on all over the world. Keeping in touch with these developments and learning how to capitalize on them is essential for survival in these revolutionary times.

The very notion of continuous improvement suggests that individuals and teams will learn from both their accomplishments and their mistakes. TQManagers help their employees to gain insights from personal experiences, and they strive to institutionalize this process so that it lets teams share with others what they have learned. In this way, TQM teams learn from their work experience, including their failures, and pass on this learning to others, creating an organization that is continuously learning and improving.

REFLECTIONS ON CREATING A LEARNING AND CONTINUOUSLY IMPROVING ORGANIZATION

Take a few moments to reflect on your organization and your own attitude toward continuous improvement and learning, using Exhibit 7.1.

THE RELEVANCE OF A LEARNING AND CONTINUOUSLY IMPROVING ORGANIZATION

The attitude of every TQM leader we've interviwed is: "We're not there yet, and we probably never will be. But we'll keep trying to do better." In the 1960s, 1970s, and early 1980s, American managers liked to say, "If it ain't broke, don't fix it." (President Reagan was still saying this in 1990.) Now it's been changed to "If it isn't perfect, improve it." This determination to continuously keep improving is a central theme in TQM.

Total Quality is a powerful strategy for improving. At Motorola they continue to press for a Six Sigma standard (3.4 defects per million) and they talk about departments that have maintained 100 percent error-free production for three and four months at a time to demonstrate that perfection is pos-

Exhibit 7.1. Reflections on a Learning and Continuously Improving Organization.

1. Think of the manager you admire the most. List three things that person did to advance your own competencies and career. Why were they important to you?

   ■ _____

   ■ _____

   ■ _____

2. Check your own behavior. How often is each of these statements true of you?

   Note: Some of these statements can be regarded as positive, others as negative.

	Almost Never	Rarely	Sometimes	Frequently	Almost Always
■ I regard my team's training as an essential element in TQM and as my responsibility.	—	—	—	—	—
■ I provide my employees with honest feedback on their performance and use this as a developmental tool.	—	—	—	—	—
■ I help my employees with their career planning.	—	—	—	—	—
■ I keep my employees advised about the organization's core competency needs.	—	—	—	—	—
■ I use my inspection of my team's quality-improvement processes as a tool for learning.	—	—	—	—	—
■ I believe that training expenses are a worthwhhile investment.	—	—	—	—	—
■ My employees' learning needs are a shared requirement between them and the organization.	—	—	—	—	—
■ I believe that sharing vital work information is more important than the "need to know" system.	—	—	—	—	—
■ I recognize people for obtaining new skills.	—	—	—	—	—
■ I keep my employees advised of all the information about our business that I can obtain.	—	—	—	—	—

After you have finished reading this chapter, return to this chart, review your responses, and make notes on how you might want to change.

sible. At Xerox they still quote David Kearns's concept of being in "a race without a finish line." However, improvement requires the complex and often painful challenge of change, and changing work practices is not easy; traditional patterns of behavior have sometimes been learned too well. They must be replaced with new learning—learning that gives everyone in the organization the tools and processes of quality.

Helping workers to learn from their mistakes is a key part of the "new learning" and the new management style of patience and a focus on incremental improvements. With PDCA (Plan-Do-Check-Act) as the means of learning more about work processes, employees and TQManagers are increasingly able to learn from their mistakes. Most breakthroughs in work activity are the result of gaining insights from personal experience, and many quality organizations are discovering that if they can institutionalize this phenomenon they can anticipate significant improvements in work processes and technological development. In an era of intellectual property, where white-collar and blue-collar workers are fast being replaced by "gold-collar" workers (persons who possess strategic knowledge), it behooves an organization to facilitate the transmission of knowledge to as many workers as possible in the shortest time possible.

One of the major breakthroughs in education in this century was a shift in focus from teaching to learning. Maria Montessori, an Italian educator working in the Netherlands, was the first to advocate this point of view. She demonstrated that schools were designed to ease the burden of teaching at the expense of learning. From her investigations she discovered much about how people learn that has significant bearing on TQM:

- Images are better than words. If a learner can see, feel, touch—in short, bring all five senses to bear on the acquisition of knowledge—learning is increased.
- Showing is better than telling.
- Too much instruction is worse than too little.

- When the stakes get too great and anxiety is high, learners tend to avoid experimentation and openness to new experiences and revert to previously successful behavior.

- Positive reinforcement of what is done right is far more effective than sanctions when things are done wrong.

A TQManager uses these insights to help her team not only to learn the skills they need to practice TQM, but also to fine-tune their interdependence as a team of learners. In his insightful book on organizational learning, *The Fifth Discipline* (1990, p. 236), Peter Senge writes:

> Team learning is the process of aligning and developing the capacity of a team to create the results its members truly desire. It builds on the discipline of developing shared vision. It also builds on personal mastery, for talented teams are made up of talented individuals. But shared vision and talent are not enough. The world is full of teams of talented individuals who share a vision for a while, yet fail to learn. The great jazz ensemble has talent and a shared vision (even if they don't discuss it), but what really matters is that the musicians know how to *play* together.

This is a key responsibility of TQManagers and a requirement of a learning organization—helping the team to know how to play together.

HELPING AND BLOCKING FACTORS FOR CREATING A LEARNING AND CONTINUOUSLY IMPROVING ORGANIZATION

A manager who wants to adopt the personal practices that will lead to a learning organization must first focus on the few vital behaviors that will best achieve this goal. At the same time he will have to be aware of the behaviors that will block his progress. (See Figure 7.1.)

HELPING FACTORS: FIVE THINGS THE TQMANAGER CAN DO

Treat Training and Learning as a Required Investment in Human Assets

TQManagers have flexibility and a willingness to learn, and they expect the same commitment from their team. They know that for training to be effective in supporting the transition to TQM it must go beyond traditional thinking about industrial training. Not only must the knowledge and skill requirements of Total Quality be taught, but learning programs that address personal and group behaviors are necessary to help individuals deal with one another as colleagues and partners in collaboration.

This learning is not without its costs. The organization will certainly invest in developing or acquiring training programs for TQM and the TQManager will provide every team the time to attend this training. But much more is required. To be successful a TQManager must see the members of her team as assets whose value to the organization can be replenished over and over again. Achieving this vision requires an investment of time and patience that allows team members to acquire required skills, personal insights about themselves and the others on the team, the competencies of a team player, and opportunities for on-the-job experiential learning.

Encourage People to Learn from Mistakes

In an environment that encourages prudent risk taking, failure can be used as a valuable learning experience. When they are viewed with the right perspective, failures are a rich, fertile

Figure 7.1. Creating a Learning and Continuously Improving Organization.

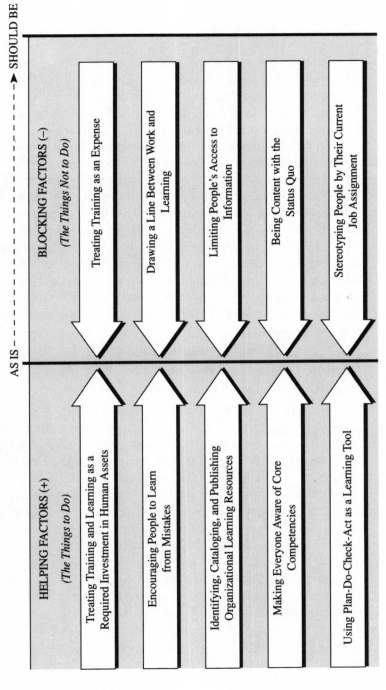

AS IS - ➤ SHOULD BE

BLOCKING FACTORS (−)
(The Things Not to Do)

Treating Training as an Expense

Drawing a Line Between Work and Learning

Limiting People's Access to Information

Being Content with the Status Quo

Stereotyping People by Their Current Job Assignment

HELPING FACTORS (+)
(The Things to Do)

Treating Training and Learning as a Required Investment in Human Assets

Encouraging People to Learn from Mistakes

Identifying, Cataloging, and Publishing Organizational Learning Resources

Making Everyone Aware of Core Competencies

Using Plan-Do-Check-Act as a Learning Tool

ground for learning that can lead to significant breakthroughs in process improvement and technological development. Failures should be studied and analyzed — not punished — to enhance the probability of success in the future.

In his famous essay, "A Dissertation upon Roast Pig," Charles Lamb describes how meat was eaten raw until, one day, the son of a Chinese villager accidentally set fire to his father's cottage and lost everything, including a litter of pigs. While sifting through the ashes and lamenting his poor fortune, the son burned his fingers on the roasted corpse of a pig. Too cool them, he put them in his mouth and discovered a wonderful new taste. Roast pig, a delicious and soon essential food source, had been found in the ashes of tragedy. Houses all over the village were soon burning right and left, until a sage used root cause analysis to provide a more reasonable means of producing roast pig.

Identify, Catalog, and Publish
Organizational Learning Resources

TQManagers are leaders who want to enable their teams to be more productive. To do so they have to provide a compilation of information regarding the technical, managerial, and quality learning opportunities available to their organization. Because it is certain that the team will require educational support beyond what is available inside the organization, TQManagers have to help the team diagnose what special or critical needs are important to their work processes and must facilitate the acquisition of this learning. This may be simply access to information about customers, work processes, or variances in production, or it may be specific technical skills or knowledge that can only be acquired by cross-training or an outside learning program. Whatever the need, it is important for the TQManager to record the needs and the kinds of experiences or programs that are available internally or externally to the organization.

Many organizations maintain more than one learning center or training department. Such organizations should publish a consolidation of all their educational offerings across functional boundaries and share them with all their employees. However, if this does not happen, TQManagers must take it upon themselves to develop these lists and catalogs and provide them to their teams. They also should work with other managers to develop lists of cross-training opportunities that represent mutual advantages.

Make Everyone Aware of Core Competencies

One of the hallmarks of TQM is the consistency with which processes and tools are applied within the organization. With consistency, everyone from the boardroom to the shop floor, from Engineering to Marketing, will speak the same language of quality improvement. Reaching this kind of consistency requires all of an organization's people to be trained using a set of core modules that support the practice of quality improvement. When an employee's work demands specialized technical skills that are not needed by the majority, only that employee should receive the relevant skill training. As an example, managers have to know the basic concepts, tools, and processes just like everyone else, but they also need to learn skills for managing the use of quality tools and for inspecting work processes, so that they can facilitate their employees' quality applications on the job.

Beyond quality, at the very heart of the organization is a set of core skills or competencies. Microsoft Corporation would not be where it is without programmers; their most important coding professionals are a group of specialists who create the most complicated code and keep Microsoft a leader in their field. American Airlines could not exist without pilots, but they also could not operate without the financial analysts who evaluate travel patterns, flight loads, and pricing to predict which routes will be profitable and which are essential to feed passengers to the longer routes. What are the core competencies in your organization? Do you have a sufficient supply of these skills? Do people in your organization know what these skills are and how to become competent in them?

Xerox began its rise to success with a dry-copy process called xerography. Xerography is not taught in schools and xerographic engineers are not graduates of colleges, nor are they abundant in other organizations from which they can be recruited. Xerox learned long ago that xerographic engineering was a core competency that was learned experientially, from one engineer to another.

Use PDCA (Plan-Do-Check-Act) as a Learning Tool

How an organization deals with problems — especially failures — says much about that organization's culture. One of Deming's key rules is: "Find problems. It is management's job to work continually on the system" (Deming, 1986). There is something healthy and inspiring about people who feel strong enough to take a steady look at a problem and ask, "What caused it?" and "How can we avoid it in the future?"

Many companies have adopted a form of product post-mortem called a Presidential Review, which can last as long as a day. The product development team (which is usually a cross-functional team) presents the history of its work against the original plan, supported by documentation; highlights the deviations from the plan, both good and bad; and identifies the cause of any deviation. It can be thought of as the Check and Act steps from Deming's PDCA circle (Figure 5.2) applied to product development. The purpose is to isolate the causes of deviations and ensure that they are communicated to other product development teams, thus providing a focus for improving development practices to ensure predictability in future programs.

Policy deployment has replaced management by objectives in most TQM organizations. Policy deployment is a three-phase process with a focus on quality improvement. The first two phases of the process, Establish policy and Deploy policy, comprise the Check-Act-Plan steps of PDCA. In the Establish phase, information from every area of the company about how to improve customer satisfaction is collected and analyzed. Senior management pulls all existing and potential new policies (objectives, operating priorities, etc.) into an organizational perspective and appoints a senior executive to develop an improvement strategy for each policy or objective. Local management does the functional evaluations and develops problem statements, measurements, and targets.

Functional management completes an analysis and countermeasures for the proposed targets as a way to confirm the initial plans. Budgeting is addressed at this point so that projects affecting the organization's improvement are included in the normal budgeting process. Senior management then reviews the revised plans and issues the final policy deployment plan to guide the organization's efforts. Local TQManagers then develop and implement plans to achieve the targets, completing the PDCA cycle.

In policy deployment, both successes and failures offer something important. Whether goals are reached or not, an analysis at year's end such as the Presidential Review should reveal opportunities for improving the process. And by incorporating the PDCA process in an objective setting, an organization can experience quality improvements and organizational learning across all aspects of its operations.

BLOCKING FACTORS: FIVE THINGS THE TQMANAGER SHOULD NOT DO

Don't Treat Training as an Expense

Someone said, "Quality begins with training, and quality ends with training." This is true — it is a continual challenge to keep on top of quality technology and maintain a work force that has the latest knowledge and skills. But training is an *investment* that provides significant returns, and it is a key pillar in any TQM strategy. The nature of the organization itself, its mission, products, and work environment, will dictate what kind of curriculum is required. As an example, production workers will not be likely to require the level of process detail that Engineering or Marketing may need. An eight-hour-a-day classroom delivery will not be operationally appropriate for all employees and more streamlined, bite-sized elements may be better for production and field personnel. And, of course, the investment must be considered. Training is not cheap and customization is one way of getting "the most bang for the buck."

Don't Draw a Line Between Work and Learning

There is little doubt that most Americans work hard. They want to work and take pride in doing high-quality work. They are highly innovative. Nor do we doubt that it is management's responsibility to create the kind of work environment where employees can bring their energy and talent to bear on their work problems. In the early days of quality, organizations that had success in creating work environments based on employee involvement and the quality of work life came to realize that greater quality and productivity improvements could be achieved by providing training in the tools and processes of Total Quality. They also discovered that much of the real learning of how TQM worked in their organizations occurred on the job in interchanges among employees. And they discovered that "making quality work" is a learning experience. Whether they are dealing with quality or specific work skills, TQManagers clearly see the connection between work and learning.

Managers know that the responsibility for development and training is a partnership between the TQM organization and the employee. Each employee is responsible for taking the initiative for his own professional development. Acquiring new skills and knowledge is a career-long process, one that must become an integral part of the work ethic of every employee in a learning organization. TQManagers are expected to assume responsibility for pursuing development and training opportunities that increase their ability to lead more effectively and are responsible for working with their employees to identify development needs, to form development plans, and to ensure that these plans are implemented in a planned and meaningful way.

Don't Limit People's Access to Information

Organizations, even TQM organizations, have a right to protect proprietary information. But in a learning organization the "need to know" system can become a barrier to learning. In our information-driven economy, competitive advantage can be found in only three areas—productivity, speed, and information or knowledge. Whether it is state-of-the-art technological information or knowledge about customers, when a team requires the information to get its job done, traditional security precautions too often slow down the work process. We live and work in an era when some employee possesses within his head the knowledge that is our strategic advantage. We cannot prevent that employee from leaving or succumbing to an accident. It is wise to be certain that his knowledge is replicated in another head, or two, or three. And knowledge breeds knowledge. When we share information we stimulate new thoughts and dialogue about how that information might be used or exploited. That is exactly what the TQManager wants to facilitate.

Don't Be Content with the Status Quo

The most valuable asset in industry today is its human capital. Fifty years ago, a high school diploma was all that was needed for factory workers and a college degree was sufficient for people who went to work in a suit and tie. But times have changed. Between now and the year 2000, virtually all jobs will require some form of lifelong learning to upgrade and maintain skills.

David Kearns, former deputy secretary of the U.S. Department of Education, when he was CEO at Xerox, said: "We want educated people who are prepared to go to work and who have learned how to think. Then we will continue to help them learn throughout their careers" (Galagan, 1990, p. 4).

Kearns's view was more universal when he wrote, with Denis Doyle in *Winning the Brain Race*, "If wealth was once measured in gold, silver, and precious stones, it is now measured in what we know. And just as gold and other forms of physical capital are portable, so too is 'human capital,' the acquired knowledge, skills, and attitudes imparted by education. It's yours for life, you are what you know" (Kearns, 1989, p. 6).

Don't Stereotype People by Their Current Job Assignment

A learning organization has to take into consideration the diversity of employee backgrounds and experiences. Employee-learners come from a variety of professions; they are auditors and systems analysts, engineers and production workers, technicians and sales representatives, professionals and paraprofessionals. They are the college-educated, the high school graduates with no math skills, the working statisticians, the interested and the uninterested. The current job of an employee does not necessarily reflect her true potential, skills, or competencies. TQManagers must recognize the diversity of their work force and determine the extent of the backgrounds and skills that are present to see how this diversity can best be used for the good of the whole team. By incorporating real-life assessments, the TQManager can motivate a diverse group to want to learn and use the tools that will broaden the team's total competence. TQManagers learn not to judge a book by its cover or employees' capabilities by their current job.

KEY BEHAVIORS THAT SUPPORT A LEARNING AND CONTINUOUSLY IMPROVING ORGANIZATION

To create a learning and continuously improving organization, the TQManager will do the following:

Continue to...

- Evaluate for performance

Do more...

- Listening to colleagues and subordinates
- Teaching and coaching
- Systems thinking
- Communicating in all directions
- Following through in a supportive, rather than an evaluative, mode
- Looking for both incremental improvements and breakthroughs in processes
- Seeing the potential value of collaboration

Do less...

- Directing and controlling

Start...

- Understanding the organization as a system of interdependent relationships
- Assuming that a successful organization must be a learning organization
- Assuming that priority attention must be given to processes
- Assuming that improvement is more important than maintenance
- Focusing on prevention by inspecting the process, rather than only the finished product
- Learning from problems

Stop...

- Excessive criticism of people for making mistakes
- Short-term thinking
- "Preaching," exhorting, and depending on the power of words alone

YOUR PERSONAL PLAN FOR CREATING A LEARNING AND CONTINUOUSLY IMPROVING ORGANIZATION

At this point it might be helpful for you to review your answers to the reflective questions in Exhibit 7.1. On the basis of our discussion about a learning and continuously improving organization and your earlier assessment, you may wish to consider steps you want to take in order to adjust your behavior. Use the form in Exhibit 7.2.

SUMMARY COMMENTS

Preparing a work force to meet current and future business objectives by providing appropriate educational and training opportunities to employees is essential to an organization in the 1990s, but especially to organizations pursuing TQM. The responsibility of the TQManager is to define the minimum training requirements that are related to the employees' roles, responsibilities, and needs, including those of customer satisfaction and quality. TQManagers also have to successfully complete their own functional knowledge and skills training to properly coach, inspect, and reinforce the work of their employees.

Dr. Gilbert Rapaille (Lader, 1988, p. 35), a quality consultant to AT&T, likens the transformation to TQM to a child's learning process. He describes a child at play in front of adults:

> He is active. Suddenly something goes wrong. He fails. He does something that does not fit the adult expectations. He cries, is upset, ashamed, and he realizes he did not know exactly what to do. Somebody is there—his teacher, his grandparents, perhaps. They say, "It's all right that you made a mistake. I care about you, because you

Exhibit 7.2. Notes on a Learning and Continuously Improving Organization.

Now that I have read the chapter on a learning and continuously improving organization and reviewed my answers to the reflections in Exhibit 7.1, there are some personal actions I want to take to ensure that I am developing my team's skills and self-sufficiency. Therefore, I will do the following:

- Continue to... _____

  _____

  _____

- Do more... _____

  _____

  _____

- Do less... _____

  _____

  _____

- Start... _____

  _____

  _____

- Stop... _____

  _____

  _____

- Seek feedback on... _____

  _____

  _____

  _____

  _____

---

are somebody special and I trust you. I'm sure you are going to get better." The child tries again and eventually succeeds. He feels good about what has happened. He is proud of succeeding, of having overcome the difficulties.

Rapaille believes that this is how TQM should work in America. He suggests that successful quality efforts recognize that results are secondary to the process and the breakthroughs that lead to success. "In fact," he says, "we could say that a result without the process is not quality. If we haven't stumbled, failed, and tried again, we haven't produced an internal feel for quality" (pp. 35–36).

RESOURCES

SHARPENING YOUR TQMANAGERIAL SKILLS

Any improvement effort—organizational or personal—begins by gathering and examining data. In the previous chapters we invited you to do some reflecting and to bring into focus experiences that you have gathered over the years. In this part you will find resources to use in your self-development. To begin, we suggest that you get some data from your colleagues about how they see you. The comparison should be very enlightening and will provide a good base from which to launch your personal improvement program.

This part also provides a glossary of TQM terms that may be useful in your discussions with colleagues, some information about TQM experts we referred to earlier, and readings to deepen your understanding of TQM and the five key TQManagerial competencies we have discussed.

We wish you well in your quest for personal and organizational excellence!

A

Getting and Using Feedback About Yourself

The most important instrument you have to work with is *you*. The one person over whom you have the most control is *you*. The one person you have the greatest responsibility to improve is *you*.

To use yourself most effectively and to improve yourself as a TQManager you need understanding, data collection, analysis, planning, and experimentation. As we think with you about how to acquire these skills, we'll draw on the experience of some successful TQManagers from many different kinds of organizations around the country. (See Exhibit A.1.)

GETTING FEEDBACK FROM SUBORDINATES AND COLLEAGUES

In addition to reflecting on your behavior from time to time, it is also useful to get feedback from those who work with you. We tend to judge ourselves by our intentions, but others judge us by our behavior. The starting point for improving your

Exhibit A.1. Understanding Yourself.

How often is each of these statements true of you? Record the numerical rating (1 to 5) that is appropriate.	Almost Never	Rarely	Sometimes	Frequently	Almost Always
	1	2	3	4	5

- I consider that keeping my subordinates and colleagues fully informed is a top priority. — — — — —

- I have full confidence in my subordinates, and I make a point of showing it. — — — — —

- I don't mind taking risks with those around me, knowing that even if we fail, we'll learn. — — — — —

- I try to make it comfortable for people to give me their honest feedback on how they view my actions. — — — — —

- I am a good listener. — — — — —

- I make a special effort to understand people who support positions with which I disagree. — — — — —

- Teams are always more creative and productive than individuals in dealing with complexity. — — — — —

- I make every effort to recognize team effort, rather than singling out individuals. — — — — —

- I take the time to document important work processes. — — — — —

- I try to make certain that we don't just solve problems, but also look for their root causes. — — — — —

- My colleagues and I set goals that are measurable. — — — — —

- Solving problems is important, but taking time to find their causes is even more important. — — — — —

- I am fair and consistent in giving appropriate recognition and rewards to the people I supervise. — — — — —

- I have given people a clear idea of what they have to do to get special recognition or rewards. — — — — —

- My colleagues and I regularly review our recognition-and-reward systems to assess their fairness and impact. — — — — —

- I am alert for new opportunities to give appropriate recognition for innovations or work well done. — — — — —

- Employees should be encouraged to take some risks and should be applauded even when those risks do not produce the desired results. — — — — —

Exhibit A.1. Understanding Yourself, Cont'd.

How often is each of these statements true of you? Record the numerical rating (1 to 5) that is appropriate.	Almost Never	Rarely	Sometimes	Frequently	Almost Always
	1	2	3	4	5
▪ I consider that training and coaching are one of my key responsibilities as a manager.	—	—	—	—	—
▪ I regard mistakes as opportunities for learning.	—	—	—	—	—
▪ My subordinates and I all know how to use the Plan-Do-Check-Act process.	—	—	—	—	—
▪ I use quality-improvement processes to review business performance and results.	—	—	—	—	—
▪ I am always open to new ideas and work processes.	—	—	—	—	—
▪ I believe that it is important for the root causes of problems to be clearly understood.	—	—	—	—	—
▪ I inspect my team's work processes, not just their results.	—	—	—	—	—
▪ I seek and value my team's input on their workload and priorities.	—	—	—	—	—
TOTAL	—	—	—	—	—

Interpreting Your Score

Instruments like this are useful only to the extent that they make us more aware of our behavior. Here is our suggestion about how to interpret your score:

100–125:   Your behavior consistently demonstrates a TQM philosophy.

75–99:   You are well on your way, but you need to focus on the areas where you are inconsistent.

74 or below: You have considerable room for improvement and need to look particularly at those items where you checked 1 or 2.

When you think about the behaviors that you "Almost Never" or "Rarely" use, you might ask yourself questions like "Why don't I do that more often?" "What might happen if I change?" "If I wanted to change, when and where would be a good place to start?" Then try the new behavior and see what happens!

management style is an honest assessment of your current behavior by people who are familiar with it. If you are interested in getting feedback from your colleagues, you can duplicate and distribute Exhibit A.2.

Remember that some subordinates may be skeptical of your intentions and just a little apprehensive. In approaching people about giving you feedback, explain that it is a chance for them to provide you with their observations about your management practices. Tell them that their candid feedback will help you to plan for change, if necessary.

MAKING USE OF FEEDBACK

After you have reviewed the results of the input by your subordinates and associates, you will want to compare their assessments with your own. It is likely that there will be areas of difference, as well as a confirmation of concerns you identified yourself. It is also likely that you will not always agree with the assessments. On those occasions you will want to clarify the input and put it into statements you can use for developmental planning.

Although you are not obligated to share the input, you may discover that this is the best way to clarify the data. Also, by involving the people who have given you the feedback, you will be better able to enlist their support in developing well-defined improvement plans. There are several different ways you can make use of the data your colleagues have provided:

- *Personal, private reflection:* Here you simply compare your responses with the same items and make note of those where there is a discrepancy. The question then becomes: "What do I do that causes people to see me so differently?"

- *Discussion with close friends or colleagues:* Ask these people to review the results and the results of your self-assessment and give you their interpretation. Then discuss the implications and develop a strategy for making any changes that are indicated.

- *Discussion with your colleagues who provided the feedback:* Here your purpose is to get a clearer picture of what you do that causes them to perceive you in a particular way. *It is critically important in this session that you do not become defensive!* It may even be useful to leave the room for a few minutes while they discuss you. This will free them to be more candid when you rejoin them. The outcome of this session may very well be a more open and trusting relationship because you have demonstrated your confidence in them and the value you place on their opinion. You can also encourage them to give feedback to one another more freely and informally in the future.

When you have finished gathering and analyzing all the inputs, you will want to translate this data into developmental action plans. In evaluating the data, focus on the two or three areas where you have the greatest developmental needs. But before you begin struggling with that, be certain that you have also identified the areas of your greatest strength. You don't want to waste time in areas where there is no need, and you want to remind yourself to keep focused on what you are doing that is working. Finally, develop plans for meeting your developmental needs. These may include plans for training, team building, individual study, and other developmental activities, as well as plans to follow up on the survey in a reasonable time. In conducting your assessment and action plan, you might want to use the Self-Assessment Summary in Exhibit A.3

USING THE EXPERIENCE OF OTHERS

While getting a clear understanding of our behavior is critical, it is also useful to learn from the experience of others. To get

Exhibit A.2. A Request for Your Observations.

This is a request for candid and anonymous feedback on how you see me doing my job. You will help with my personal continuous improvement program if you will check the columns below and return this sheet to me in an unmarked envelope. With thanks for your candor:

Signature: _____

	Almost Never	Rarely	Sometimes	Frequently	Almost Always
Directions: *Think of describing the person whose name appears on this sheet to a friend. How often is each of these statements true of this person?*					
■ Gives top priority to keeping colleagues and subordinates fully informed.	—	—	—	—	—
■ Has full confidence in subordinates and makes a point of showing it.	—	—	—	—	—
■ Doesn't mind taking risks with others, knowing that even if we fail, we'll learn.	—	—	—	—	—
■ Tries to make it comfortable for people to give their honest feedback on how they view his or her actions.	—	—	—	—	—
■ Is a good listener.	—	—	—	—	—
■ Makes a special effort to understand people who support positions with which he or she disagrees.	—	—	—	—	—
■ Believes that teams are always more creative and productive than individuals in dealing with complexity.	—	—	—	—	—
■ Makes every effort to recognize team effort, rather than singling out individuals.	—	—	—	—	—
■ Takes the time to document important work processes.	—	—	—	—	—
■ Tries to make certain that we don't just solve problems, but also look for their root causes.	—	—	—	—	—
■ Sets goals that are measurable.	—	—	—	—	—
■ Believes that solving problems is important, but that taking time to find their causes is even more important.	—	—	—	—	—
■ Is fair and consistent in giving appropriate recognition and rewards to the people he or she supervises.	—	—	—	—	—
■ Gives people a clear idea of what they have to do to get special recognition or rewards.	—	—	—	—	—

Exhibit A.2. A Request for Your Observations, Cont'd.

	Almost Never	Rarely	Sometimes	Frequently	Almost Always
Directions: *Think of describing the person whose name appears on this sheet to a friend. How often is each of these statements true of this person?*					
■ Regularly reviews recognition-and-reward systems to assess their fairness and impact.	—	—	—	—	—
■ Is alert for new opportunities to give appropriate recognition for innovations or work well done.	—	—	—	—	—
■ Encourages employees to take some risks and is supportive even when those risks do not produce the desired results.	—	—	—	—	—
■ Regards training and coaching as one of his or her key responsibilities as a manager.	—	—	—	—	—
■ Regards mistakes as opportunities for learning.	—	—	—	—	—
■ Knows how to use the Plan-Do-Check-Act process.	—	—	—	—	—
■ Uses quality-improvement processes to review business performance and results.	—	—	—	—	—
■ Is open to new ideas and work processes.	—	—	—	—	—
■ Believes that it is important to clearly understand the root causes of problems.	—	—	—	—	—
■ Inspects a team's work processes, not just their results.	—	—	—	—	—
■ Seeks and values team members' input on their workload and priorities.	—	—	—	—	—

Thank you!

Source: TQManager: A Practical Guide for Managing in a Total Quality Organization, by Warren H. Schmidt and Jerome P. Finnigan. Copyright © 1993 by Jossey-Bass Publishers. Permission to reproduce and distribute material (with copyright notice visible) is hereby granted. If material is to be used in a compilation to be sold for profit, please contact the publisher for permission.

an idea of what successful people have learned, we did a survey as part of our preparation for this book. It was not a scientific sample; we asked colleagues from large and medium-sized public and private organizations from Massachusetts to Cal-

Exhibit A.3. Self-Assessment Summary.

Areas of greatest strength:

_____

_____

_____

_____

_____

_____

_____

Areas of greatest need:

_____

_____

_____

_____

_____

_____

Plans for meeting my developmental needs:

_____

_____

_____

_____

_____

_____

_____

ifornia to tell us about their experience. We asked them, "What advice would you give to managers in organizations that are becoming—or are about to become—TQManaged?" Here are some of their responses:

- "Establish long-term goals for your organization."
- "Establish sincere values."
- "Get senior managers on board."
- "Implement the team concept; work at team motivation."
- "Show respect for the work force."
- "Work on role modeling."
- "Figure out early who your malcontents will be."
- "Measure everything."
- "Focus on documenting results to prove it will work."
- "Implement TQM in total; TQM is not a buffet where managers pick and choose what they are willing and able to do."
- "Involve as many employees as possible in establishing goals."
- "Involve your union."
- "Learn the concept of the internal customer."
- "Begin slowly."

These same experienced TQManagers had recommendations of what *not* to do:

- "Don't be too hasty."
- "Don't take the slogan approach."
- "Don't cave in to the 'hard sells.'"
- "Don't try to take personal credit."
- "Don't expect it to happen overnight just because you call it Total Quality."

- "Don't ignore labor unions and employee organizations."
- "Don't stampede training."
- "Don't try to spread it too quickly."
- "Don't separate TQM planning, leadership, and operations from business planning, leadership, and operations."
- "Don't get bogged down in the Total Quality bureaucracy that can develop."
- "Don't skip formal training."
- "Don't turn an organization into figures alone."

A 1992 study of national quality award–winning organizations and quality consultants (Ramirez, 1992) found that the three most important contributors to a successful TQM effort, in order of importance, are:

1. Management commitment and support, actively demonstrated
2. A focus on customer satisfaction
3. A clear vision, or purpose statement, supporting quality improvement

THE BOTTOM LINE: THE SUCCESSFUL TQMANAGER IS A LEARNING MANAGER

In a world of constant change, the only formula for success is to keep learning. The successful manager alternates between doing and learning. Every new action is a hypothesis to be tested. You try something, watch, and assess the results; you then reflect on why it happened that way. Every event is viewed as a potential for learning. In that spirit, before you put this book away, it is important that you capture the oppor-

Exhibit A.4. My Personal Plans.

As a result of reading *TQManager*, I'm going to take the following actions:

I will . . .	By . . .

tunities for learning you have discovered. Exhibit A.4 provides a simple format you can use to portray the actions you plan to take to become a TQManager. We congratulate you on your commitment and wish you the best for a rich future in a quality world!

Glossary of TQM Terms and Tools

Appraisal costs: costs associated with inspecting a product to ensure that it meets specifications.

Benchmarking: measuring your own products, services, and practice against the best in the field. Benchmarks usually include a measure of results and an analysis of the process used to produce those results.

Best of class: when an organization, function, product, process, or component is superior to all comparable ones.

Brainstorming: technique used to generate ideas. Most commonly used in groups, its object is to gather as many ideas as possible in a specific time frame.

Cause: an established reason for the existence of an event.

Cause-and-effect diagram: a graphic technique describing the cause of a specific outcome (also known as a fishbone diagram or Ishikawa diagram). The cause-and-effect diagram (Figure B.1) is useful to display all the possible causes of a specific problem or condition. Dr. Kaoru Ishikawa is credited with inventing cause-and-effect analysis. The problem, or effect, is stated on the right side of the chart and the major influences, or causes, are listed to the left. The diagram illustrates the various causes affecting a process by sorting and relating them. For every effect there are likely to be several major categories of causes (the bones of the fish). The major causes are usually listed as the "Four M's": manpower, machines, methods, and material (although any major category that helps people think creatively can be used). The fishbone takes shape as possible causes are listed on each of the major bones. The objective is to cure the cause and not merely list the symptoms. There are four key steps in constructing a cause-and-effect diagram:

1. Begin by agreeing on the effect (problem statement).
2. Generate the causes by check-sheet data or brainstorming.
3. Place the problem statement in a box to the right, draw the four major cause categories (or the steps in the work process), and add brainstormed ideas. For each cause, ask, "Why does this happen?"

Figure B.1. Cause-and-Effect Diagram (Fishbone or Ishikawa Diagram).

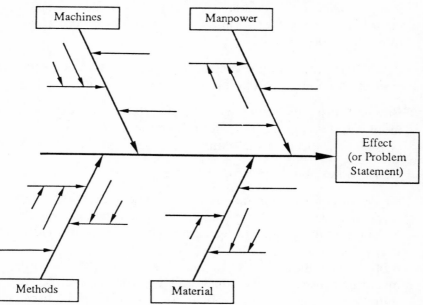

4. Identify the root (most basic) causes of the problem by finding the factors that are repeated. Collect additional data to verify the relationship of causes to effect.

Check sheet: a tally sheet (Figure B.2) to gather data based on sample observations in order to identify patterns. This is the logical starting point in most problem-solving cycles. A check sheet is an easy-to-understand method of learning how often certain events happen. Constructing a check sheet involves four steps:

1. Agree on what you want to know. (Everyone on the team has to be looking at the same thing.)
2. Decide on the most reliable way to collect the data.
3. Design a format for recording data.
4. Make sure time is available for gathering the data.

Figure B.2. Check Sheet.

Problem	Month			
	1	2	3	Total
A	‖	‖	│	5
B	│	│	│	3
C	⊬⊦⊦	‖	⊬⊦⊦	12
Total	8	5	7	20

Common cause: see Random variation.

Control: The set of activities used to detect and correct deviation in order to maintain a desired condition.

Control chart: a graphic way (Figure B.3) to discover how much variability in a process is due to random variation and how much is due to unique events, as a means of determining if a process is in statistical control. Control charts were developed by Walter Shewhart in the 1920s, but it was W. Edwards

Deming who perfected their use. Deming's research with control charts led him to his conclusion that 85 percent of improvement opportunities come from changes in the system, which is management's responsibility, while only 15 percent are within an individual employee's control. A control chart is simply a run chart with statistically determined upper control limit (UCL) and lower control limit (LCL) lines on either side of the process average. The limits are calculated by allowing a process to run untouched, sampling the process, and plugging the sample averages into the appropriate formula. Then sample averages are plotted onto a chart to determine if these points fall within or outside of the limits, or if they form "unnatural" patterns. If either of these conditions exists, the process is "out of control." The fluctuation of points within the limits results from variation in the process, indicating common causes within the system; these can only be corrected by changing the system. Points outside of the limits usually come from special causes or exceptions to how the process normally operates. Such special causes must be eliminated before a control chart can be used as a monitoring tool. Only when special causes are corrected can the process be "in control"; sampling will make sure that the process doesn't fundamentally change. There are two types of control charts:

1.   *Variable control chart:* Samples are expressed in quantitative units of measurement, such as length, weight, and time.
2.   *Attributes control chart:* Samples reflect qualitative characteristics, such as "is defective/is not defective" or "go/no go."

Corrective action: implementation of solutions that result in the elimination of identified problems.

Cost of quality: the sum of the cost of prevention, appraisal, and failure. A financial tool that can be used as an indicator of variation, as well as a measure of productivity and efficiency.

Cross-functional teams: teams whose members are from several different work units that interface with one another.

Figure B.3. Control Chart.

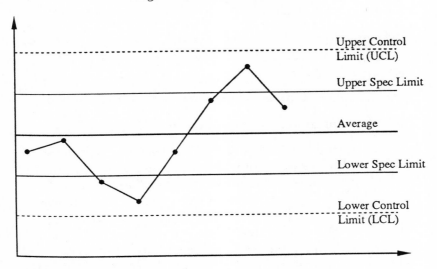

Helpful when work units are dependent upon one another for materials, information, and so on.

Culture: the prevailing pattern of beliefs, behaviors, attitudes, and values of an organization.

Customer: the recipient of the outputs of a body of work, or the purchaser of the organization's product or service.

Data: information or a set of facts presented in descriptive form. Data is either measured (variable data) or counted (attribute data).

Defect: output that fails to meet customer requirements or your own specifications (if they are higher).

Deming Prize: medal presented annually to companies that demonstrate a high level of quality. The prize was instituted by the Japanese Union of Scientists and Engineers to recognize and stimulate continuous improvement in Japan, and to honor W. Edwards Deming for his contributions toward Total Quality in Japan. (Only one American company—Florida Power and Light—has ever won the Deming Prize.)

Effectiveness: how closely an organization's output meets its goal and/or the customer's requirements.

Efficiency: production of required output at a perceived minimum cost, measured by the ratio of the quantity of resources expended to plan.

Error: the result of failing to correctly perform an action.

Fishbone diagram: see Cause-and-effect diagram.

Flow chart: a pictorial representation showing all of the steps of a work process (Figure B.4). Flow charts are helpful for identifying deviations between the actual and ideal paths of any product or service. They provide excellent documentation that can be a useful tool for evaluating how the various steps of a process relate to one another, as well as uncovering loopholes that are potential sources of trouble. Flow charts can be used to document anything from the route of an invoice or the flow of materials to the steps in a sales cycle or servicing of a product. There are three steps in developing a flow chart:

1.   Identify the major activities to be completed and decisions to be made.

Figure B.4. Flow Chart.

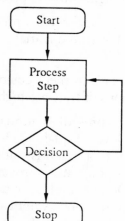

2. Use the simplest symbols possible.
3. Check the logic of the plan by following all the possible routes through the chart to ensure that you have planned for all contingencies.

Force field analysis: a technique for identifying the forces for and against a certain course of action or condition, sometimes called the helping and hindering forces. Since change is a dynamic process, suggesting movement from time A to time B or from condition X to condition Y, it is appropriate to examine where the energy for this movement comes from. One approach is to view change as the result of a struggle between forces seeking to upset the status quo—"driving forces" that move a situation toward change while "restraining forces" block the movement. When the opposing forces are equal or the restraining forces are too strong to allow movement, there is no change. It stands to reason that some change will occur when the driving forces are more powerful than those on the restraining side. Force field analysis (Figure B.5) was developed by Kurt Lewin to help groups facilitate change in three ways: (1) by encouraging people to think together creatively about all the facets of a desired change, (2) by helping people to reach consensus about the relative priority of factors on each side of the "balance sheet," and (3) by providing a starting point for action.

Frequency distribution: the count of the number of occurrences of individual values over a given range (discrete variable) or the count of events that lie between certain predetermined limits over the range of values the variable may assume (continuous variable).

Functional administrative control technique: a tool designed to improve performance through a process combining time management and value engineering. The process involves breaking activities down into functions and establishing teams to target and solve problems in each function.

Histogram: a bar graph showing the frequency with which events occur by displaying their distribution. A histogram

Figure B.5. Force Field Analysis.

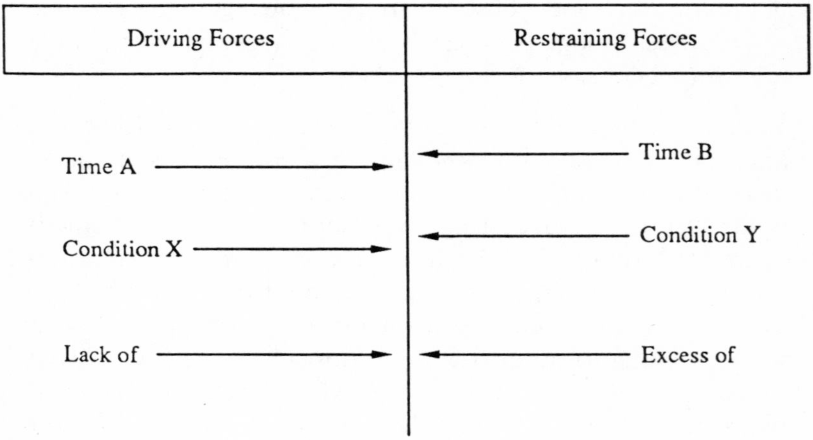

Driving Forces	Restraining Forces

Time A ⟶   ⟵ Time B

Condition X ⟶   ⟵ Condition Y

Lack of ⟶   ⟵ Excess of

(Figure B.6) shows the distribution of data by bar graphing the numbers of units of anything in separate categories. As with a Pareto diagram, a histogram displays in bar-graph form the frequency with which events occur, but it goes beyond Pareto by taking measurement data and displaying its distribution; this is critical since the repetition of events will produce results that vary over time. Since random samples of data under statistical control normally follow the pattern of the bell-shaped curve, the shape of a histogram's distribution is helpful. The first thing a histogram can show is the positive or negative deviation from normal, or *skewness*, of the curve. It can also show *variability*, or how much spread there is in the curve. Histograms start with an unorganized set of numbers, followed by four steps:

1. If data is not already arranged by frequency, make a check sheet.
2. Determine the range (R) for the entire data set by subtracting the smallest value in the set from the largest value; divide the range value into a certain number of classes (K); determine the class width (H) by $H = R/K$; and determine the class boundary, or end points. Take

Figure B.6. Histogram.

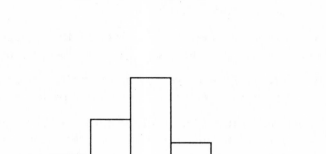

the smallest individual measurement in the data set and add the class width to it. Consecutively add the class width to each class boundary until the correct number of classes is obtained.

3. Construct a frequency table based on the values computed in step 2.

4. Using the frequency distribution table, construct vertical bars for each of the values, with height corresponding to frequency.

Ishikawa diagram: see Cause-and-effect diagram.

Kaizen: Japanese term used to describe continuous improvement in all aspects of an organization's operations at every level. It is usually thought of as a staircase in which each step upward is followed by a period of stability, followed by another step upward, and so on. Each improvement is usually accomplished at little or no expense.

Management by fact: management process in which actions and decisions are based on facts and data, not opinions. Requires (1) asking appropriate questions; (2) correctly interpreting answers to verify the quality of the data and facts; and

(3) verifying the correct use of data, facts, and statistics in the work process and in decision making.

Mean time between failures (MTBF): the average time between successive failures of a given product or process.

Measurement: the process of measuring to compare results to requirements (a quantitative estimate of performance).

Nominal group technique: a tool for idea generation, problem solving, mission description, key result-area definition, performance-measure definition, and goal-objective definition.

Normative performance-measurement technique: technique that incorporates structured group processes so that work groups can design measurement systems suited to their own needs.

Output: the specified end result, as required by a customer.

Pareto diagram: bar graph showing where scarce resources should be applied to reap the greatest gain. A Pareto diagram (Figure B.7) is used to display the relative importance of problems or conditions in order to choose the starting point for problem solving, identify the basic cause of a problem, or monitor a solution. This tool named for Vilfredo Pareto, a nineteenth-century economist, was made popular by Joseph M. Juran. It is a special form of vertical bar graph designed to help determine which problems to solve and in what order to solve them. A Pareto diagram based upon check sheets or other forms of data collection helps to direct attention and effort to the critical problems. The use of Pareto diagrams has given rise to the "80-20" rule, which suggests that 80 percent of an organization's problems come from 20 percent of its tasks. Constructing a Pareto diagram requires nine steps:

1. Use a check sheet or "brainstorm" to obtain data.
2. Arrange the data in order from the largest category to the smallest.
3. Calculate the total.

Figure B.7. Pareto Diagram.

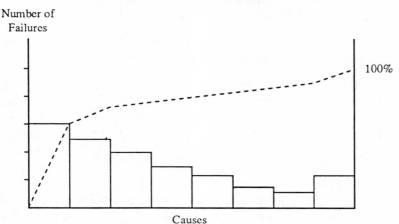

Causes

4. Compute the percentage of the total that each category represents.
5. Compute the cumulative percentage.
6. Scale the vertical axis for frequency (zero to total).
7. From left to right, construct a bar for each category, with height indicating the frequency. Start with the largest category and add them in descending order (combine the categories containing the fewest items into an "other" category and put it on the extreme right, as the last bar).
8. Draw a vertical scale on the right and add a percentage (0 percent to 100 percent) scale.
9. Plot a cumulative percentage line.

Policy: a statement of principles and beliefs, or a settled course, adopted to guide the overall management of affairs in support of a stated aim or goal.

Policy deployment: the interactive development of strategies, goals, objectives, and plans and the communication, implementation, and process capability assessment of these strategies, goals, objectives, and plans. Benchmarking data is a critical enabler for policy deployment, which is focused primarily on the process and the organizational system.

Prevention: a future-oriented approach to quality management that achieves improvements through corrective action.

Problem: a question or situation proposed for solution, or the effect of not conforming to customer requirements.

Problem-solving model: a step-by-step process for moving from problem definition to problem resolution. It is in the context of a systematic problem-solving process that the application of statistical tools most commonly occurs. By using a standard problem-solving process (Figure B.8), regardless of the functional background of the team members, an organization enjoys a common method and language for analyzing variabilities, determining true causes, and planning optimal solutions. The operation of cross-functional problem-solving teams and the general management of problem resolution are therefore more easily facilitated by having all employees use the same process. There are many problem-solving models in use by America's quality leaders; all of these models are designed to offer a systematic approach to resolving questions, issues, or problems by allowing employees to focus on three activities: (1) to conduct careful analysis based on numerical and other data and to explore potential solutions, (2) to plan for the implementation of optimal solutions, and (3) to monitor the results of their corrective actions. A typical problem-solving process follows six steps:

1. Identify and select a problem to solve.
2. Analyze the problem.
3. Generate potential solutions.
4. Select and plan a solution.
5. Implement the solution.
6. Evaluate the solution.

Process: a series of operations or activities linked together to provide a result that has increased value.

Process capability: the ability of a process to achieve the desired end result of meeting the customer's requirements.

Figure B.8. Problem-Solving Model.

Process control: the activities employed to detect and remove special causes of variation in order to maintain or restore stability.

Process flow analysis: a technique for identifying and analyzing key processes and areas and methods of possible improvement.

Process improvement: activities employed to detect and remove common causes of variation in order to improve process capability.

Productivity: ratio of outputs produced to inputs required (an expected outcome of Total Quality).

Quality: those attributes of a product or service that the customer values. May include surface finish, functionality, timeliness, size, cost, reliability, or other factors.

Quality circles: a group of workers and their supervisor who voluntarily meet to identify and solve job-related problems.

Quality function deployment (QFD): a technique to build customer requirements into a product design or service process to ensure that customer requirements are met (sometimes called the House of Quality).

Quality improvement process: a process of continuous quality improvement that provides a road map the organization can follow to keep headed in the direction of producing quality products and services. It shows where to begin and what questions to ask along the way in order to stay on track. It helps keep the focus on customer requirements and avoids costly side trips and wasteful backtracking. The emphasis is on continuous improvement, rather than results, because this approach focuses employee creativity and innovation on the work processes that produce quality products and services, and on identifying ways to improve them. What a problem-solving process is to problem resolution, a quality-improvement process is to meeting customer requirements; it helps employees change the way they do their work to improve the quality of the services and products they provide their internal or external customers. Regardless of the process used, quality improvement is approached from the viewpoint of the supplier who is responsible for producing the work, while remembering that suppliers are also customers for someone else's work. The power of a quality-improvement process lies in this kind of open communication between supplier and customer and in their shared responsibility. The steps in this continuous quality improvement process are

1.   Identify the work to be done.
2.   Identify the customer for the work, using real names.

3. Identify the customer's requirements in a dialogue.
4. Convert customer requirements into the supplier specifications required and renegotiate with the customer as necessary.
5. Identify a work process that will meet the requirements.
6. Select measurements for the critical steps in the process.
7. Determine the capability of the process to deliver the expected outcomes.
8. Evaluate the results and identify steps for improving the process.
9. Decide on the next steps.

Quality of work life: the degree to which an organization's culture provides employees with information, knowledge, authority, and rewards to allow them to work safely and effectively, be compensated fairly, and maintain human dignity in their work.

Random variation: variation in a process output that is usually the result of *common* causes that can often only be improved by management (in contrast to *special* causes, which the employee using the process may address).

Range: the difference between the maximum and minimum values of data in a sample.

Reliability: the probability that a product entity will perform its specified function under specified conditions, without failure, for a specified period of time.

Requirement: a formal statement of need and the expectations of how it is to be met (what the customer wants).

Root cause analysis: a process of eliminating myriad effects and causes to reach the bottom line of a problem — the primary reason for the problem or symptom (sometimes called first cause analysis).

Run chart: The simplest possible display of trends within observation points over a specified period of time (Figure B.9). Run charts are most often used to monitor a system to deter-

Figure B.9. Run Chart.

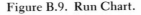

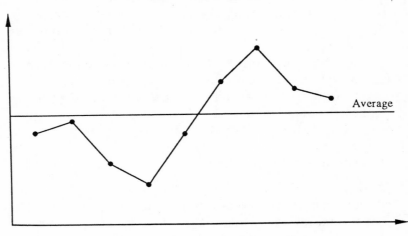

mine if the long-range average is changing. Points are plotted on the graph in the order in which they become available. Typical examples of processes that can be graphed are machine downtime, yield, scrap, typographical errors, and productivity over time. There is a caution: be alert to the tendency to see every variation in data as significant. The purpose of a run chart is not to identify all problems, but to focus attention on the truly vital changes in the system.

Scatter diagram: a diagram consisting of a horizontal axis representing the measurement values of one variable and a vertical axis representing the measurements of a second variable (Figure B.10). Events are plotted and used to test for correlations and possible cause-and-effect relationships. Although it cannot prove that one variable causes another, it does help to show whether a relationships exists and the strength of the correlation. There are three steps to building a scatter diagram:

1.   Collect 50 to 100 paired samples of related data and construct a data sheet.

Figure B.10. Scatter Diagram.

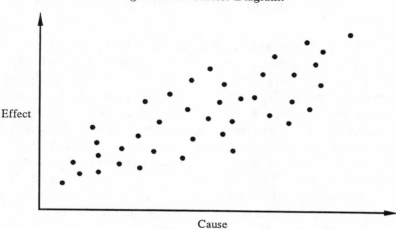

2. Draw the horizontal and vertical axes of the diagram, increasing values as you move up and to the right on each axis. Place the cause variable on the horizontal axis and the effect variable on the vertical axis.

3. Plot the data on the diagram and circle the values that are repeated as many times as appropriate.

Seven management tools: tools used to solve problems when data is not readily available, must be rearranged, or is taken from subjective descriptions rather than data bases. Typically used to solve management-level problems. Tools include (1) relational diagrams, (2) affinity diagrams, (3) tree diagrams (4) matrix diagrams, (5) matrix data-analysis diagrams, (6) PDPCs (process decision program charts), and (7) arrow diagrams.

Simulation: the technique of observing and manipulating an artificial mechanism (model) that represents a real-world process that for technical or economical reasons is not suitable or available for direct examination.

Six Sigma: statistical measure of variability of near perfection used by Motorola and other TQM companies. Permits only

3.4 deviations (errors) per million, which is 99.9997 percent perfect.

Six Steps to Six Sigma: Six Sigma is Motorola's quality-measurement system (Norling, 1989), where *t* means virtually zero defects. Sigma indicates how often defects are likely to occur; the higher the Sigma level, the lower the defect rate. As an example: 1 Sigma = 32 percent defect rate, 2 Sigma = 5 percent defect rate, and 6 Sigma = .0000002 percent defect rate or 3.4 defects per million. This metric is used in all Motorola operations and has become their only true measure for defect elimination. To help Motorola's operations reach Six Sigma levels, they devised a six-stage methodology called Six Steps to Six Sigma, a process not unlike the nine-step quality-improvement process. The methodology is used proactively in two ways. First, it is used to prevent defects before they can occur — that is, to change the way work is done so that defects are not produced. Second, it is used to anticipate customer requirements. As performance improves, customer expectations rise, and the definition of a defect becomes increasingly stringent. Implicit in the Six Steps to Six Sigma methodology is this ongoing iteration:

1. Identify the product or service you provide.
2. Identify the customer for your product or service, and determine what is considered important by that customer.
3. Identify your need to provide a product or service that satisfies the customer.
4. Define the process for doing the work.
5. Make the process mistake-proof and eliminate wasted effort.
6. Ensure continuous improvement by measuring, analyzing, and controlling the improved process.

Special cause: a source of variation in the process output that is unpredictable, unstable, or intermittent (also called assignable cause).

Standard deviation: a parameter describing the spread of the process output, denoted by the Greek letter sigma. The positive square root of the variance.

Statistic: any parameter that can be determined on the basis of the quantitative characteristics of a sample. There are two kinds of statistic: (1) *descriptive* — a computed measure of some property of a set of values, making possible a definitive statement about the meaning of the collected data — and (2) *inferential* — indicating the confidence that can be placed in any statement regarding its expected accuracy, the range of its applicability, and the probability of its being true. Consequently, decisions can be based on inferential statistics.

Statistical process control (SPC): application of statistical techniques for measuring and analyzing the variation in processes.

Statistical quality control (SQC): application of statistical techniques for measuring and improving the quality of processes. Includes diagnostic tools, SPC, sampling plans, and other statistical measures.

Statistical tools: graphic and/or numerical mathematical methods that assist in analysis of a process or population of things. The seven most commonly used are (1) check sheets (or tally sheets), (2) cause-and-effect diagrams, (3) histograms, (4) Pareto diagrams, (5), control charts, (6) scatter diagrams, and (7) run charts.

Statistics: the branch of applied mathematics that describes an analysis of empirical observations for the purpose of predicting certain events in order to make decisions in the face of uncertainty.

Strategy: a broad course of action, chosen from a number of alternatives, to accomplish a stated goal.

Suppliers: individuals, teams, or organizations that provide input to a work group or customer. Suppliers are internal or external.

Ten times improvement (10 × Improvement): reducing the error rate to one-tenth of its existing rate.

Timeliness: the promptness with which quality products and services are delivered relative to the customer's requirements.

Total Quality Management (TQM): Cooperative form of operating an organization in a way that relies on the talents of both labor and management to continually improve quality and productivity using teams and facts in decision making.

Variable: a data term to identify values within some range that appear with a certain frequency or pattern.

Variance: in quality management terminology, any noncon-formance to requirements. In statistics it is the square of the standard deviation.

C

TQM Experts and Publications
You Should Know About

THE BEST-KNOWN
TQM EXPERTS

Crosby, Philip B.: founder of the Quality College in Winter Park, Florida, and author of *Quality Is Free* and *Quality Without Tears*. Among the first quality professionals to hold a senior management position (vice president of quality for ITT Corporation) and the first of the American quality gurus to become well known. Credited with being the creator of zero defects, he developed a fourteen-step quality-improvement process that is the basis for many quality-improvement programs. Crosby emphasizes "cost of quality" (see Feigenbaum) and estimates that American companies spend more than twenty cents of every sales dollar on making mistakes, finding them, and fixing them. For service companies the cost of quality can be as high as thirty-five cents of every sales dollar.

Deming, W. Edwards: world's best-known quality expert. Trained as a statistician, he worked for Western Electric in the 1920s and 1930s. During World War II he taught quality-control techniques to companies that produced military goods. He introduced statistical concepts and quality concepts to the Japanese beginning in 1950. He told them that it is impossible to "inspect" quality into finished goods, stressing the need to prevent mistakes by using quality-control charts all along the production line. Deming's research with control charts led him to conclude that about 85 percent of the opportunities for improvement come from changing the system, which is management's responsibility. Only about 15 percent of the improvement opportunities are within the individual employee's control. He achieved fame at the age of eighty, following the television documentary, *If Japan Can, Why Can't We?* Deming advocates constancy of purpose and control of variances to achieve quality and believes in releasing worker power by creating joy, pride, and happiness in work. He is most famous for his fourteen points for management.

Feigenbaum, Armand V.: author and lecturer on quality. Feigenbaum was the manager of worldwide manufacturing operations and quality at General Electric Company. He coined the term *total quality control* (1956) and is recognized as the inventor of cost of quality. Feigenbaum categorizes quality into four jobs: new design control, incoming material control, product control, and special process studies.

Ishikawa, Kaoru: one of Japan's leading quality experts. Ishikawa was a leader of the Japanese Union of Scientists and Engineers (JUSE), and is recognized as the father of quality circles and employee empowerment. He edited JUSE's handbook, *Quality Control for Foremen*, which is a guide for establishing and maintaining quality circles. He is most famous for being the inventor of cause-and-effect analysis. See Cause-and-effect diagram.

Juran, Joseph M.: codeveloper of the first statistical process control techniques for manufacturing while employed at Bell Laboratories' Hawthorne Works in 1924. His book, *The Quality Control Handbook*, was published in 1951 and became a quality bible in the United States and Japan; however, his work was better received in Japan. His work and lectures influenced the Japanese to expand quality to include an overall concern for the entire management of an organization. In 1966 Juran predicted that the Japanese would achieve world leadership in quality and introduced quality circles to the United States with an article entitled "The Quality Circle Phenomenon." Juran defines quality as fitness for use and advocates a project approach to quality improvement. He is perhaps best known for teaching the Pareto principle, which he named after Vilfredo Pareto.

Shewhart, Walter: person credited with the first application of statistical concepts to production and the development of control charts, when he was a statistician with Bell Laboratories in the 1920s. Shewhart authored two books that had a profound effect on Deming—*Economic Control of Quality of Manufactured Product* and *Statistical Method from the Viewpoint of Quality Control.* It was based on Shewhart's teaching that Deming developed his PDCA (Plan-Do-Check-Act) cycle.

Taguchi, Genichi: noted for developing an approach to quality engineering (the Taguchi method) that uses designed experiments to improve product and process quality. The objective is to achieve a robust design that is insensitive to uncontrollable factors such as usage and environment and to minimize variations around a target parameter. Taguchi also developed the loss function concept, which allows a quantitative estimate to be made of the loss due to variability. His methods are taught and used in product development throughout the world.

BOOKS YOU SHOULD KNOW ABOUT

Overview of TQM

Bowles, J., and Hammond, J. *Beyond Quality.* New York: Putnam, 1991. A history of the quality movement in the United

States, including examples from fifty American companies, and a persuasive argument for focusing on continuous improvement and using the Baldrige Award as an assessment of progress, not an objective.

Collins, F. C., Jr. *Quality: The Ball in Your Court.* Milwaukee, Wis.: American Society for Quality Control, 1987. Examines a course of action to improve quality by reviewing the experiences of dozens of foreign and domestic firms.

Crosby, P. *Quality Is Free: The Art of Making Quality Free.* Milwaukee, Wis.: American Society for Quality Control, 1979. Shows how doing things right the first time adds nothing to the cost of a product or service.

Crosby, P. *Quality Without Tears: The Art of Hassle-Free Management.* Milwaukee, Wis.: American Society for Quality Control, 1984. Covers Crosby's fourteen-step plan for fighting the secret enemies of quality, developing a quality culture, and getting all employees to commit to quality.

Crosby, P. *Let's Talk Quality: 96 Questions You Always Wanted to Ask.* Cincinnati, Ohio: Association for Quality and Participation, 1989. Looks at the major issues in quality improvement and management in a question-and-answer format, including what quality really means, how to get it, what quality standards should be, and how quality should be measured.

Davis, S. *Managing Corporate Culture.* New York: Ballinger, 1984. Describes the connection between corporate culture and strategy, the difference between dealing with "guiding beliefs" and "daily beliefs," and how the executive can go about changing the culture of an organization.

Davis, B. L., Hellervick, J. L., Sheard, J. L. (eds.), *Successful Manager's Handbook.* Minneapolis, Minn.: Personnel Decisions, Inc., 1989. Contains specific development suggestions for thirty-nine management skill areas and Personnel Decisions, Inc.'s (PDI) Management Skills Profile (MSP), an assessment tool that provides feedback on management skills.

Deming, W. E. *Out of the Crisis.* Milwaukee, Wis.: American Society for Quality Control, 1986. Deming's statement of what American managers have been doing wrong and what they must do to correct the problem—features the famous fourteen points.

Dertouzos, M., Lester, R., and Solow, R. *Made in America.* Cambridge, Mass.: MIT Press, 1989. Identifies what is best and worth replicating in American and international industrial practices and sets out five national priorities for regaining the productive edge.

Desatnick, R. L., and Detzel, D. *Managing to Keep the Customer: How to Achieve and Maintain Superior Customer Service Throughout the Organization.* (2nd ed.) San Francisco: Jossey-Bass, 1993. Describes how to achieve and maintain superior customer service.

Dobyns, L., and Crawford-Mason, C. *Quality or Else: The Revolution in World Business.* Boston: Houghton Mifflin, 1991. A companion book to the IBM-funded PBS series, *Quality or Else.* Explains the ideas and innovations of the quality management philosophy. Argues that America must start working toward a quality-based culture or take a back seat in the global economy.

Feigenbaum, A. V. *Total Quality Control.* Cincinnati, Ohio: Association for Quality and Participation, 1983. Tells how to plan a quality program and set up an appropriate organizational structure to implement it.

Garvin, D. A. *American Business: A Two-Minute Warning.* New York: Free Press, 1988. Identifies ten major changes American managers must make to revive American productivity and growth and to bolster the quality of American products and services.

Garvin, D. A. *Managing Quality: The Strategic and Competitive Edge.* Milwaukee, Wis.: American Society of Quality Control, 1988. Describes eight dimensions of quality: performance, features, reliability, conformance, durability, service-ability, aesthetics, and perceived quality.

Hunt, V. D. *Quality in America: How to Implement a Competitive Quality Program*. Homewood, Ill.: Business One Irwin, 1992. Analyzes the present state of the practice of quality in America and shows how to successfully implement a competitive quality program based on the Quality First methodology.

Imai, M. *Kaizen: The Key to Japan's Competitive Success*. New York: McGraw-Hill, 1986. Presents sixteen management practices that support *Kaizen* — the gradual, unending improvement to achieve ever higher levels of quality in an organization.

Ishikawa, K. *What Is Total Quality Control? The Japanese Way*. Cincinnati, Ohio: Association for Quality and Participation, 1985. Explains how to produce higher-quality goods at lower costs by applying quality control at every stage of market research, design, production, and sales.

Ishikawa, K. *Guide to Quality Control*. Cincinnati, Ohio: Association for Quality and Participation, 1986. Contains chapters on the basic statistical techniques used by quality circles and discusses several less familiar techniques.

Juran, J. M. *Juran on Planning for Quality*. Milwaukee, Wis.: American Society for Quality Control, 1988. Outlines Juran trilogy — quality planning, quality control, and quality improvement.

Juran, J. M. *Juran on Leadership for Quality: An Executive Handbook*. Milwaukee, Wis.: American Society for Quality Control, 1989. Provides managers with specific methods they need to successfully lead their companies on a quest for quality and discusses how to apply planning, control, and improvement to quality leadership.

Kearns, D., and Nadler, D. *Prophets in the Dark: How Xerox Reinvented Itself and Beat Back the Japanese*. New York:

HarperCollins, 1992. Describes the global challenge to Xerox products and markets beginning in the 1970s, the decision to transform the corporation to a Total Quality company, and the company's success in regaining market share from Japanese competitors.

Mann, N. R. *The Keys to Excellence: The Story of the Deming Philosophy*. Los Angeles: Prestwick Books, 1987. Provides guidelines for senior executives and managers to transform their organizations to become more competitive in the global marketplace.

Peterson, D., and Hillkirk, J. *A Better Idea: Redefining the Way Americans Work*. New York: Houghton Mifflin, 1991. The former CEO of Ford Motor Company shows how you can revitalize a company by driving responsibility down and tapping the creativity in all employees.

Rosander, A. C. *The Quest for Quality in Services*. Milwaukee, Wis.: American Society for Quality Control, 1989. How to plan and start a service quality program. Describes the work of five experts and their influence on services, plus the eight kinds of knowledge needed for improvement of quality, and tells how to conduct a continuous customer-opinion survey.

Scherkenbach, W. W. *The Deming Route to Quality and Productivity: Roadmaps and Roadblocks*. Washington, D.C.: Ceepress, 1986. Written by the man who guided Ford Motor Company's implementation of Deming's philosophy, this book is a readable account of Deming's fourteen points in action.

Schmidt, W., and Finnigan, J. *The Race Without a Finish Line*. San Francisco: Jossey-Bass, 1992. Based on interviews and site visits with twelve Baldrige Award–winning companies, as well as two President Award winners. Provides a complete guide to implementing TQM in any organization — private or public.

U.S. General Accounting Office. *Management Practices: U.S. Companies Improve Performance Through Quality Efforts*. Gaithersburg, Md.: U.S. General Accounting Office,

May 1991. Reports on the impact of TQM practices on the performance of twenty U.S. companies that were among the highest-scoring applicants in 1988 and 1989 for the Malcolm Baldrige National Quality Award.

Vaill, P. B. *Managing as a Performing Art: New Ideas for a World of Chaotic Change.* San Francisco, Calif.: Jossey-Bass, 1989. Presents new solutions to deal with the unprecedented challenges brought on by changes in technology, increasingly volatile markets, and intensified foreign competition.

Walton, M. *The Deming Management Method.* Cincinnati, Ohio: Association for Quality and Participation, 1986. Explains Deming's fourteen points and examines the results attained by some of America's most innovative firms.

Walton, M. *Deming Management at Work.* New York: Putnam, 1990. Offers practical applications of the Deming management method. Several successful practitioners of the method are profiled.

Zemke, R., and Schaaf, D. *The Service Edge: 101 Companies That Profit from Customer Care.* New York: NAL Books, 1989. Profiles 101 companies that benefit from superior service and provides analysis of successful service policies and procedures.

Openness and Trust

Block, P. *The Empowered Manager: Positive Political Skills at Work.* San Francisco: Jossey-Bass, 1987. Describes how to put positive political skills to work to maintain personal and organizational vitality.

Carlzon, J. *Moments of Truth.* New York: Ballinger, 1987. Tells the story of the turnaround of Scandinavian Airlines Systems and describes how SAS empowered employees to solve customer problems — "the moments of truth."

Guaspari, J. *I Know It When I See It: A Modern Fable About Quality.* New York: American Management Association, 1985. Short story intended to guide managers to a new understanding of what quality really is and how to achieve it.

Guaspari, J. *The Customer Connection: Quality for the Rest of Us.* New York: American Management Association, 1987. Explores, with humor, why quality got such a bad name in this country, why it is hard to meet quality objectives, and the customer-supplier relationship.

Collaboration and Teamwork

Barry, T. J. *Quality Circles: Proceed with Caution.* Milwaukee, Wis.: American Society for Quality Control, 1988. Examines quality circles through twenty-eight years of management experience with IBM.

Hackman, J. R. "The Design of Work Teams." In J. W. Lorsch (ed.), *Handbook of Organizational Behavior.* Englewood Cliffs, N.J.: Prentice-Hall, 1984. Describes tools and processes for establishing teamwork and employee involvement.

Kayser, T. A. *Mining Group Gold: How to Cash in on the Collaborative Brain Power of a Group.* El Segundo, Calif.: Serif, 1990. Presents tools that emphasize teamwork and the building of consensus through careful planning and facilitation.

Scholtes, P. R., and others. *The Team Handbook.* Madison, Wis.: Joiner and Associates, 1989. A how-to book with guidelines for making project teams more effective in using data-centered methods to improve processes.

Shonk, J. H. *Team-Based Organizations.* Irwin, Ill.: Business One, 1992. Teams and teamwork are the buzzwords of the early 1990s; this book describes means for instituting a team system in an organization.

Tichy, N. M., and Devanna, M. A. *The Transformational Leader.* New York: Wiley, 1990. Presents an integrated set of concepts and practical technologies for managing strategic reorientations in products, services, markets, organizational structure, and human resource systems.

Managing by Fact

Gitlow, H., and Gitlow, S. *Deming Guide to Quality and Competitive Position.* Cincinnati, Ohio: Association for Quality and Participation, 1987. A how-to guide to improving quality and productivity in any type of organization. Discusses Deming's fourteen points as well as labor's corollary eleven points that integrate management's and labor's efforts.

Gitlow, H., Gitlow, S., Oppenheim, A., and Oppenheim, R. *Tools and Methods for the Improvement of Quality.* Homewood, Ill.: Irwin, 1989. Introduces statistical tools and quality-improvement processes and ties them to the Deming management philosophy.

Harrington, H. J. *The Improvement Process: How America's Leading Companies Improve Quality.* Cincinnati, Ohio: Association for Quality and Participation, 1987. Reviews what has been done in the United States to improve quality. Also explains how to start, evaluate, and improve a quality program.

Harrington, H. J. *Business Process Improvement.* New York: McGraw-Hill, 1991. Presents what has to be done to improve business processes by the principles of continuous improvement.

Hart, M. K., and Hart, R. *Quantitative Methods for Quality and Productivity Improvement.* Milwaukee, Wis.: American Society for Quality Control, 1989. Explains the need for continuous improvement, presents the statistical methods for process control, and shows limitations and alternatives.

Hradesky, J. L. *Productivity and Quality Improvement.* New York: McGraw-Hill, 1988, Describes a twelve-step productivity process for quality improvement and statistical process control.

Messina, W. *Statistical Quality Control for Manufacturing Managers.* New York: Wiley, 1987. Provides a practical guide to tools and techniques for improving quality, increasing productivity, and enhancing the competitive position of a manufacturing line.

Mills, C. *The Quality Audit: A Management Evaluation Tool.* Milwaukee, Wis.: American Society for Quality Control, 1989.

Examines the quality audit process from the viewpoints of the person requesting an audit, the organization being audited, and the auditor carrying out the audit.

Mizuno, S. *Management for Quality Improvement: The Seven New QC Tools*. Cambridge, Mass.: Productivity Press, 1988. Explains seven new quality tools that promote a higher level of quality-control activity, total coordination of the workplace, and creative planning.

Mizuno, S. *Company-Wide Total Quality Control*. Tokyo: Asian Productivity Organization, 1989. Describes essentials of a company-wide Total Quality control program, including the manager's role, functions of quality assurance, product liability, cross-functional management, and quality-control audits.

Ozeki, K., and Asalea, T. *Handbook of Quality Tools: The Japanese Approach*. Norwalk, Conn.: Productivity Press, 1990. Offers a discussion of the management aspects of quality and reviews the seven basic quality-control tools and five new tools.

Wheeler, D. J., and Chambers, D. *Understanding Statistical Process Control*. Knoxville, Tenn.: SPC Press, 1986. Uses case histories and a variety of graphs to explain how SPC techniques work.

Recognition and Rewards

Beer, M., Spector, B., Lawrence, P. R., Melle, D. Q., and Walton, R. E. *Managing Human Assets*. New York: Free Press, 1984. Discusses a variety of considerations in establishing recognition-and-reward systems.

Blanchard, K., and Johnson, S. *One Minute Manager*. New York: Morrow, 1982. An easily read story that quickly shows three very practical techniques for managing people with feedback and praise.

Lawler III, E. E. *Strategic Pay: Aligning Organizational Strategies and Pay Systems*. San Francisco: Jossey-Bass, 1990. Methods of reward systems and their connection to organizational goal setting and achievement.

Lawler III, E. E., Ledford, G. E., Jr., and Mohrman, S. A. *Employee Involvement in America: A Study of Contemporary Practice.* Houston: American Productivity and Quality Center, 1989. An overview of employee involvement schemes and the value of recognition-and-reward planning.

Mohrman, A. M., Jr., Resnick-West, S. M., and Lawler III, E. E. *Designing Performance Appraisal Systems: Aligning Appraisals and Organizational Realities.* San Francisco: Jossey-Bass, 1989. Strategies and procedures for establishing appraisal-and-reward systems that fit organizational goals.

O'Dell, C. *People, Performance and Pay.* Houston: American Productivity and Quality Center, 1989. The significance of recognition and reward in motivation.

The Learning and Continuously Improving Organization

Conger, J. A. *Learning to Lead: The Art of Transforming Managers into Leaders.* San Francisco: Jossey-Bass, 1992. Describes the skills and tools necessary for managers to become effective leaders in the 1990s.

Nadler, D. A., Gerstein, M. S., Shaw, R. B., and Associates. *Organizational Architecture: Designs for Changing Organizations.* San Francisco: Jossey-Bass, 1992. Describes strategies and models for establishing organizational strategies for continuous improvement, learning organizations, and high-performance work systems.

Senge, P. R. *The Fifth Discipline: The Art and Practice of the Learning Organization.* New York: Doubleday, 1991. Discusses five key component technologies for the excelling organization of the future.

REFERENCES

Blanchard, K., and Johnson, S. *One Minute Manager*. New York: Morrow, 1982

Bradford, D., and Cohen, A. *Managing for Excellence: The Guide to Developing High Performance in Contemporary Organizations*. New York: Wiley, 1984.

Carlzon, J. *Moments of Truth*. New York: Ballinger, 1987.

Crosby, P. *Quality Is Free: The Art of Making Quality Certain*. New York: McGraw-Hill, 1979

Culbert, S., and McDonough, J. *Radical Management: Power-Politics and the Pursuit of Trust*. New York: Free Press, 1985.

Deming, W. E. *Out of Crisis*. Cambridge, Mass.: MIT Center for Advanced Engineering Study, 1986.

Dertouzes, M. L., Lester, R. K., and Solow, R. M. *Made in America*. Cambridge, Mass.: MIT Press, 1989.

Drucker, P. *Innovations and Entrepreneurship*. New York: HarperCollins, 1985.

Federal Quality Institute. *Introduction to Total Quality Management in the Federal Government*. Washington, D.C.: U.S. Office of Personnel Management, 1991.

Feigenbaum, A. V. "Total Quality Control." *Harvard Business Review*, Nov. 1956.

Galagan, P. A. "A CEO's View of Training." *Training and Development Journal*, May 1990.

Ginnodo, W. "Abstract of TQM History and Principles." *Tapping the Network Journal*, Quality & Productivity Management Association, Spring–Summer 1991.

Grayson, C. J., and O'Dell, C. *American Business: A Two-Minute Warning*. New York: Free Press, 1988.

Harrington, J. H. *Business Process Improvement*. New York: McGraw-Hill, 1991.

Houghton, J. "The Chairman Doesn't Blink." *Quality Progress*, March 1987.

Imai, M. *Kaizen: The Key to Japan's Competitive Success*. New York: McGraw-Hill, 1986.

Juran, J. *Juran on Leadership for Quality*. New York: Free Press, 1989.

Kaplan, R. *Beyond Ambition: How Driven Managers Can Lead Better and Live Better*. San Francisco: Jossey-Bass, 1991.

Kayser, T. A. *Mining Group Gold: How to Cash in on the Collaborative Brain Power of a Group*. El Segundo, Calif.: Serif, 1990.

Kearns, D. T. *Values and Direction*. Stamford, Conn.: Xerox Corporation, 1991.

Kearns, D. T., and Doyle, D. P. *Winning the Brain Race: A Bold Plan to Make Our Schools Competitive*. San Francisco: ICS, 1988.

Lader, J. "Getting Emotional About Quality." *Quality Review*, Summer 1988.

Lamb, C. "A Dissertation Upon Roast Pig." In J. Ball (ed.), *From Beowulf to Modern British Writers*. New York: Odyssey Press, 1959.

Likert, R. *The Human Organization*. New York: McGraw-Hill, 1967.

Livingston, J. S. "Pygmalion in Management." *Harvard Business Review*, July–August 1969, pp. 81–89.

MacFarland, M. "The Concept of Doing It Right the First Time." *Washington Technology*, March 22–April 4, 1990.

McGregor, D. *The Human Side of Enterprise*. New York: McGraw-Hill, 1960.

Naisbitt, J., and Aburdene, P. *Re-inventing the Corporation.* New York: Warner, 1985.

Naval, M. "Total Quality Management in the Health Care Industry." Paper prepared for the U.S. Office of Management and Budget, 1989.

Rummler, G., and Brache, Alan P. "Managing the White Space." *Training,* Jan. 1991.

Schmidt, W. H., and Finnigan, J. P. *The Race Without a Finish Line: America's Quest for Total Quality.* San Francisco: Jossey-Bass, 1992.

Senge, P. M. *The Fifth Discipline: The Art and Practice of the Learning Organization.* New York: Doubleday, 1990.

Thurow, L. *Head to Head: The Coming Battle Among Japan, Europe and America.* New York: Morrow, 1992.

U.S. General Accounting Office. *Management Practices: U.S. Companies Improve Performance Through Quality Efforts.* Gaithersburg, Md.: U.S. General Accounting Office, May 1991.

Vaill, P. B. *Managing as a Performing Art: New Ideas for a World of Chaotic Change.* San Francisco: Jossey-Bass, 1989.

Walton, M. *The Deming Management Method.* New York: Perigee, 1986.

INDEX